INTERRUPTION INSURANCE

PRACTICAL ISSUES

by

Gordon J.R. Hickmott,
M.B.E., F.C.I.I., F.C.I.Arb.

Books by Gordon Hickmott:
   Principles and Practice of Interruption Insurance
   Interruption Insurance: Proximate Loss Issues

All rights reserved. No part of this publication may be reproduced, stored in a retrieval system or transmitted in any form or by any means, electronic, mechanical, photocopying, recording, or otherwise, without permission of the publisher and copyright owner

While the principles discussed and the details given in this book are the product of careful study, the author and publisher cannot in any way guarantee the suitability of recommendations made in this book for individual problems, and they shall not be under any legal liability of any kind in respect of or arising out of the form or contents of this book or any error therein, or the reliance of any person thereon.

INTERRUPTION INSURANCE

PRACTICAL ISSUES

by

GORDON J.R. HICKMOTT,
M.B.E., F.C.I.I., F.C.I.Arb.
Interruption Insurance Consultant

LONDON

WITHERBY & CO LTD.
32-36 Aylesbury Street,
London EC1R OET

First Edition
Published 1999

WITHERBY

PUBLISHERS

©

Gordon Hickmott 1999

ISBN 1 85609 180 5

All rights reserved

Printed and Published by
Witherby & Co. Ltd
32-36 Aylesbury Street,
London EC1R OET
Tel: (0171) 251 5341
Fax: (0171) 251 1296
E-mail books@witherbys.co.uk
www.witherbys.com

FOREWORD

Said at the opening of the first Parliament of Queen Elizabeth I, 1558.
"Doeth not the wise merchant in every adventure of danger give part, that he may have the rest assured." - Sir Nicholas Bacon

The importance of Interruption Insurance to the commercial world, big or small, national or multi-national, is today an accepted fact.

The many facets of commerce and industry, and the speed of change in a modern world, have combined to bring about an increasing need for clarity and agreement between Underwriters and Insured [and their advisers], to be authoritatively recorded for the benefit of all, at inception and at essential periodic review dates, and when a claim is being processed.

The standard textbooks deal with the principles but the practical day-to-day needs of the changing scene require current attention. In 1990 a booklet, "Proximate Loss Issues" was published and called for a reprint indicating the level of interest involved. Now a further booklet "Practical Issues" is available dealing with further aspects and law cases relevant to this area of insurance.

The same Author, Gordon J. R. Hickmott, M.B.E., F.C.I.I., F.C.I.Arb. has prepared the new work, a known expert in this field of whom The Hon. Mr. Justice Phillips in a draft judgement said "He is the acknowledged doyen of business insurance with the benefit of some 50 years professional experience. He is the author of a book on the topic and I was provided with a copy of this."

This new work is therefore essential to all those involved in this class of insurance whether as Underwriters, Insured or advisers to them, and those involved in the processing of claims whether Accountants, Loss Adjusters or Assessors, company claims officials or Solicitors or legal advisers and Barristers called in to assist.

While the "Millennium bug" is a new feature and no legal cases have yet arisen, a Date Recognition Clause has been circulated in the market to deal with what is termed "the M2K" problem. There are issues, it seems from the reading of this clause, that will arise if it is followed generally unchanged and these need to be addressed.

A "Supplement" has been added to this work to cover this subject to the extent possible from a wording that has been issued by a major insurer. It deals only with the material damage and interruption insurance aspects and will need to be reviewed when final wordings are fully known and the extent, that in real life, the problem turns out to be.

PREFACE

Commerce and industry do not operate to provide the insurance world with premium income. Insurance companies do not exist to act as finance houses. Insurance is intended to be the hand maiden of industry and we forget it at our peril.

Interruption insurance, whether referred to as such or by one of the older titles - consequential loss, loss of profit, or loss of revenue, etc. or its' synonym business interruption, which title more correctly refers to the counterpart cover available that operates in the U.S.A, is now widespread in its use and application throughout the world.

The principles applying in the U.K. to this separate class of insurance have evolved since its' introduction some 100 years ago. As such, they still stand today, and in my textbook "Principles and Practice of Interruption Insurance" these are fully set out and discussed. However, this form of insurance involves considerations of the ever-changing commercial, economic and social features of life; and the technological and scientific advancements that are the feature of the modern world. These all involve continued and detailed consideration to ensure the maintenance of adequate insurance protection.

Thus alterations to the policy wordings, or the introduction of agreed extension memoranda, or perhaps of "market practice" rulings being issued, will need to be faced.

Because of the normal time factors, but more importantly the non-existence of the former Consequential Loss Committee from whence agreed comments on such aspects were frequently issued, usually after consultation with the interested parties, there is no longer adequate or relevant comment etc. on such matters.

Recently there have been a number of Law cases that have given rise to important awards, but in some, unusual or mis-typed wordings have been involved. The extent that such abnormalities gave rise to the decisions made are not obvious or recorded therein.

The understanding of others may be confused by articles such as that appearing in The Chartered Insurance Institute Journal of May 1997, headed "A point of interest", explaining that the Author backs a dissenting opinion in a legal case in the Court of Appeal, without making reference to the fact that he was wishing to apply the precedent rules of " material damage" insurance to this separate class of interruption insurance. This not only suggested that the two classes of insurance required the same rules but it introduced nonsensical provisions being applied to interruption insurance covers.

This booklet is intended to deal with these current matters and with others that the Author has found, from time to time to give rise to disputes often resolved outside the Courts or in arbitration and thus not reported.

INTRODUCTION

"What is education? A parcel of books? Not at all, but intercourse with the world, with men, and with affairs".- Edmund Burke 1729-1797.

"The subject matter of the contract of insurance is money, and money only. The subject matter of insurance is a different thing from the subject matter of a contract of insurance. The subject matter of insurance may be a house or other premises in a fire policy....These are the subject matter of insurance but the subject matter of the contract is money and money only. The only liability of the insurance company is to pay money" - Brett L.J. in Rayner v Preston [1881]

    A.   Title and classes of insurance of properties.

It is from the second quotation in the heading above that is is possible to set these out clearly and avoid the confusion that often exists from various headings used in the past. The subject matter of the contract of property insurances can be divided as follows:

[1]   Property in general
[2]   Specific property such as:
        [a]   Marine - ships, cargo, freight etc.
        [b]   Motor and other vehicles
        [c]   Aircraft etc.
        [d]   Livestock - horses, cattle etc.
        [e]   Plant and machinery and electronic equipment etc.

and then the subject matter of the insurance will determine the class of insurance concerned:

        [i]   General property damage (thus called material damage as a class and not the outdated term "fire").
        [ii]   Interruption trading loss (thus called Interruption Insurance as a class and accepting the replacement of terms such as "Profits", "Consequential Loss", "Gross Profits", etc).
        [iii]   Marine
        [iv]   Motor
        [v]   Aviation
        [vi]   Livestock
        [vii]   Engineering

and the use of these terms has been adopted accordingly throughout this work.

In the U.S.A. interruption insurance policies may be on one of the several U.S.A. forms, and these incorporate different principles and practice to those of the U.K. In most other parts of the world interruption insurance contracts generally follow the practice and principles that are found in England. However, some variations do apply but rarely relative to matters that are discussed in this work. The Law that applies outside the U.K. will often vary but again, except for the U.S. A. not usually relative to that discussed herein. World-wide contracts are usually only found for the very large international operating companies and for these individual attention is essential.

To provide adequately, and to give proper professional skill and assistance to their clients, Insurance Brokers, Advisers, Legal and Accounting organisations now frequently offering services in this field, and Loss Adjusters and Assessors all need clarity in the policy contracts that are issued. Such clarity also is needed in the intentions of the parties in the arrangements made and the extent of the cover finally agreed. Standard wordings allow the work of these advisers to be expedited; individual wordings may well obviate this and introduce confusion.

I have therefore provided as Section 1, an overall reminder of the basic policy cover and its' principles and then developed a summary of the matter under which any interruption insurance claim should be prepared and then presented with attached notes outlining the adjustments arising. Subsequently further Sections deal with specific current issues that may need to be addressed.

It is to be hoped therefore, that this work will assist all parties to achieve their intentions mutually without subsequent disagreements arising and with the Underwriter realising from inception the extent of that cover for which he has given protection.

    B.   Intention of this Book.

The thrust of this work relates to interruption insurance contracts. Of necessity, reference has to be made to material damage covers as there is often no modern technical insurance work that provides the required comments or guidance thereon.

CONTENTS

	Page
Preface	vi
Introduction	vii

Section 1.
A reminder of the Principles of the basic UK policy cover — 1

A. General policy — 1

B. Specific factors — 4

  1. Problems relating to the use of figures — 4

  2. Variations of results between sections or separate activities of the business — 5

  3. Outside events not arising directly from the damage but affecting the results of the business. — 8

    [a] Events that arise only because of the insured damage — 8
    [b] Aspects that arise from damage to property surrounding that insured but not involving damage to the insurer's own property — 9
    [c] An outside event that is excluded by the policy terms — 9
      [i] a peril — 9
      [ii] a type of event — 10
      [iii] a class of property excluded — 11
      [iv] a failure to meet a policy requirement — 11

  4. Interruption loss aggravated by further damage — 12
    [a] at the insured premises but not associated with an existing insured loss — 12
    [b] at premises other than the insurer's own but which prejudices an existing insured loss — 12

  5. Losses arising from more than one event of which only one is insured — 12

  6. Factors which affect the business in consequence of production or other like changes — 12

  7. Government, public or other authorities regulations, tax changes etc. — 14

  8. Weather or holiday period considerations — 15

	9.	Lack of finance or ability to recover from the damage	16
	10.	Other miscellaneous items	18
		[a] Payments on account	18
		[b] Residual value	19
		[c] Misunderstandings re savings	20
		[d] Interest payable and revenue from claim payments	21
		[e] Policy cover relative to employees and their rights	22
		[f] So called "Consequential losses" and wherein indemnity normally lies	22
C.	Summary and Conclusions		22

Section 2.
The "Material Damage" provisions — 25

Section 3.
The meaning of the term "Premises" — 29

Section 4.
The application of "Non Disclosure" — 33

Section 5.
The "Alteration of Risk" policy condition — 39

Section 6.
A change in participation of insurers during the currency of the policy — 41

Section 7.
Contribution "Double Rent Covers" — 43

Supplement.
"M2K" or Millennium "bug" matters — 45

APPENDICES

I	The standard "recommended" U.K. Interruption Insurance Policy	57
II	Extracts from a small business "packet" policy	63
III	The legal meaning of the term "Market Practice"	95
IV	Some general notes re "Disclosure" given by the author in a Report to the High Court	97

TABLE OF LAW CASES — 101

INDEX — 105

SECTION 1

A REMINDER OF THE PRINCIPLES OF THE BASIC U.K. POLICY COVER.

"A policy of assurance is not a perfect contract of indemnity. It must be taken with this qualification, that the parties may agree beforehand in estimating the value of the subject assured, by way of liquidated damages, as they may in any other contract of indemnity." - Irving v Manning [1847] Judge Patteson.

There would appear to be no difference in principle between an agreement on a valuation and an agreement on a method of valuation, or a formula for calculating the indemnity payable.

A. GENERAL POLICY

1. The cover under a U.K. standard Interruption Insurance policy involves:
    (a) Setting out clearly the protection that the contract provides, the policy reference by title, whichever one is adopted, does not establish this adequately.
    (b) The manner by which a loss will be assessed.

2. In *Booth (Henry) & Sons v The Commercial Union Assurance Co. Ltd.* [1923], Greer J. said;

    "It is the common practice in policies of this kind, in order to prevent lengthy disputes as to what the actual loss is, that there shall be an agreed method of ascertaining that loss. It is good business and good sense to have a method which can be readily applied without difficulty and without raising a great number of points of dispute."

3. In *Elcock v Thomas* [1949], a property fire policy, in which a clause appeared agreeing the value of the interests insured Morris J., said;

    "When parties have agreed upon a valuation, then in the absence of fraud or of other circumstances, invalidating their agreement, they have made an arrangement by which for better or worse, they are bound...When losses occur after the parties to contracts have agreed upon valuations, then in some cases advantages may occur to the Insured while in other cases advantage may occur to the Insurer."

4. The current U.K. normal interruption insurance policy provides:

    "...during the period of insurance and in consequence the business carried on by the Insured at the Premises being interrupted or interfered with then the Insurer will pay to the Insured the amount of loss resulting from such interruption or interference provided that:

    a   [material damage proviso]
    b   [maximum liability limit]

This policy incorporates the Schedule, Specification and Endorsements which shall be read *together as one contract."*

In the Schedule are normally found the definitions relating to the actual case, i.e. The Insurer, Insured, etc. and usually the maximum insured indemnity period.

The perils insured will be set out as appropriate to the case.

5. The standard specification to an U.K. Interruption Insurance policy sets out:
   "The insurance under item No 1 is limited to loss of Gross Profit due to:
   (a) Reduction in Turnover and
   (b) Increase in cost of working and the amount payable as indemnity there under shall be:
   [i] in respect of Reduction in Turnover (a formula)
   [ii] in respect of Increase in Cost of Working (specific provisions)
   with then provisos re savings and under insurance."

THUS THERE NEEDS TO BE EITHER A REDUCTION IN TURNOVER OR AN INCREASE IN COST OF WORKING, OR BOTH, TO THE INSURER'S BUSINESS FOR THE POLICY THEN TO COMMENCE TO OPERATE.

6. It is usual for the specification also to include a provision for the current Auditors of the Business to be able to provide the data from the accounts thereof required by the formula under 5(a) above and for these figures to be accepted *prima facie* as such. The reasonable cost so charged by them will be recoverable under the policy. The auditors will not be paid for advice or for other services arising.

   Unless the insurers, or the appointed loss adjuster, state clearly in advance that they will accept the data uncertified, usually because they can check the figures themselves without difficulty or delay, it is not a requirement for prior permission to be obtained for such use of the Auditors.

7. It will be clear that once the interruption has arisen and this is established as at 5(a) above, then the action as indicated thereunder is to be initiated. The calculations are factual and will also establish *ipso facto* the indemnity period. The application of the other circumstances provision is a subsequent and separate matter.

8. The application of this provision arises by the action of the party who seeks to invoke it, and the "onus of proof" arising therefore falls on that party. If not established the loss adjustment is as then established by the policy formula. The adjustments will comprise alterations to figures but may give rise then to a review of the indemnity period that is to apply. It is to be noted that if only the insured had to prove matters under this provision and be made to refute insurers submissions thereunder the comments made by the Judge in the case set out in paragraph 2 would be incorrect and the purpose of the Standard Wording frustrated. *[Booth (Henry) & Sons v Commercial Union* (1923).

9. The "other circumstances" provision is incorporated by adding as bracketed clausing the following to the definitions of (a) Gross Profit (b) Annual Turnover - except if the policy is on a "Declaration linked" basis and (c) Standard Turnover.

"To which such adjustments shall be made as may be necessary to provide for the trend of the Business and for variations in or other circumstances affecting the Business either before or after the damage which would have affected the Business had the damage not occurred, so that the figures thus adjusted shall represent as nearly as may be reasonably practical the results which would have been obtained during the relative period after the damage."

10. The intention of the cover to be strictly as calculated by the formula and this to be the indemnity payable under the policy, only subject then to the "other circumstances provision," was reinforced when, in 1939, the then standard interruption insurance policy was the subject of a major review, and the current form introduced. Previously under the older form (called the Ascertained Basis Wording), in the opening clause (a) [see 5 above] the preceding words were:

"Loss of profits sustained during the period of indemnity in consequence of the within mentioned interruption or interference, but not exceeding........"

"This last limit was dropped possibly in consequence of the comments of J. Branson in the case of *Polikoff v North British and Mercantile Insce. Co. Ltd.* [1936], who said:

"It seems to me that only one calculation is desired. You are to get at the loss of profits, which are not to exceed the ascertained percentage. If after calculating the ascertained percentage it could be shewn that for some reason completely unconnected with the fire the firm in question could not have made anything like the profits which the ascertained percentage would give, the insurance company might rely upon the earlier words of clause [a]."

11. The following broad headings are set down to indicate the type and details of matters that can give rise to adjustments under the provision in question. Each is then discussed further later.

    [a] The figures themselves whether of the previous year or those within the actual indemnity period.
    [b] The variation of results between sections or departments of the business.
    [c] Outside events not arising from the damage but affecting the results of the business.
    [d] Losses arising from more than one event of which only one is insured.
    [e] Factors which affect the business in consequence of production or other like changes.
    [f] Government, Public or other Authorities regulations or tax changes.
    [g] Weather or holiday period changes.

[h] Lack of finance or ability to recover from the physical damage.
[i] Other miscellaneous items

In any individual case, care is needed to apply not the general overall aspect, for example the trend of one years' results against another year without review of the individual factors involved within the comparative figures; or that of an industry, trade or geographical area which may not be appropriate to the actual business.

B. SPECIFIC FACTORS

1 Problems relating to the comparison and use of figures

Accountancy aspects

The use of computers and modern accounting procedures while capable of control in normal trading circumstances, may not be able to be relied upon after a business is suffering from dislocation in consequence of insured damage, loss of, or damage to records or inability to collect revenue from turnover. It can be found therefore that prior to the comparisons being made, the basic factors of the imputs, timing and up-to-datedness of the relevant data have to be reviewed so that the figures to be used belong to the correct accounting periods and are accurate thereto.

Because of the interference from damage, goods sold may have the receipts therefrom posted in the ledgers (computer counterpart) later than usual so that [i] the prior damage turnover is under-stated and the post damage turnover overstated. This, it can be seen, has a double effect in reducing the reduction in turnover that applied. Loss of records insofar as book debts are concerned should be the subject of a separate insurance. Generally the outstanding amount of book debts is a capital aspect of the business as the trading, or sale, has been completed and the income relates to completed sales at the time of the damage. The revenue from Hire Purchase etc. sold goods is also not current trading income within the normal standard interruption insurance terms of the insured business. In areas of trading involving exports or imports it is necessary to consider the timing of the despatch/sale transfer inwards/outwards of the products and the invoicing/debiting of them. Again the policy is concerned with effect of the damage on trading from the date of the damage and not the time that accountancy activates the action record. In normal annual accounts the constant treatment in these matters year by year may mean that for practical purposes no adjustment is needed but when the effect on trading is to be considered often for an indemnity period of less than one year, these considerations and adjustments to rectify, may be significant to the result.

These adjustments are not matters relative to the "other circumstances provisions" as such, although it is to give effect to the basis of that provision. The normal definition used to define Gross Profit includes the usual provisions regarding opening and closing stocks, and if appropriate work in progress and sub-division between raw materials and completed stock. Whilst minor valuation adjustments between the opening and closing dates may be insignificant and are frequently ignored, technically such changes introduce a capital gain or loss in the period in question. The material damage insurance on these stocks is intended to provide indemnity at the time of the damage and thus the interruption insurance does not need to include this paper gain or loss; (or actual if stocks are liquidated against the normal level, unless this is a normal business activity involving the sale of business assets which would be prejudiced by insured damage to the premises and is thus part of the policy cover).

In industries such as oil, chemical, petrochemical and Fuel etc. and in those involved in natural products and derivatives therefrom such as wool, cotton and man-made fibres etc. there can be massive valuation changes to these assets and, whether sold or held, massive gains or losses may be introduced into the annual accounting statement. As indicated, this gain or loss should be protected by the material damage insurance and it is not a trading matter for interruption insurance purposes.

2 Variations of results between sections or departments of a business.

At one time a "Departmental clause" was added to the interruption policy to allow the Insured the option of using department figures when presenting the claim. This gave the insurers no basis for such an adjustment as it did not fall within the terms of the then "special circumstances" clause. It was not a special circumstance. There were also other aspects which could in equity call for consideration but excluded as in the case in question they were not "special" but "normal" practice to that business, such as free benefits to employees and discount vouchers applicable to only part of the trading activity. To clarify the matter the word "special" was removed and substituted by the word "other". Thus the adjustment, if established as being appropriate is available to be incorporated in the loss calculation.

Departmental Clause wording:

"If the business be conducted in Departments, the independent trading results of which are ascertainable, the provisions of Clauses [a] and [b] of items 1 shall apply separately to each Department affected by the damage, except that:

If the sum insured be less than the aggregate of the sums produced by applying the Rate of Gross Profit for each Department of the Business, whether affected by the damage or not, to the relative Annual Turnover thereof, the amount payable under item 1 shall be proportionately reduced."

Where there is a separate item on "Remuneration/Wages" a similar addition is made. If this further item is on the "Dual Basis" it must be realised that the percentages and periods set out therein will each apply to each Department and if a varied proportion was required then the remuneration item would itself need to be sub-divided.

It was once considered that it was only rarely that the accounts of a business would be in such a form that the necessary sub-division would be possible. This, however, is no longer true when the definition of "Gross Profit" is on the difference basis. The listing of the included standing charges under the older "Additions" method could give rise to the aspects of allocation of these to individual sections of a business but the newer basis requires only the very limited "non included" costs, usually clear variable expenses, to be considered. Thus the net figure for each section or department of a business can normally be easily established.

The use of section or department figures arises only when the interruption is not at a level effect over the whole activities of a business for the whole of the indemnity period.

Salvage sales

It is not unusual, with the object of reducing the possible material damage loss and the associated trading loss, to arrange for a special sale after the insured event. This is in respect of undamaged, semi-damaged or suspect goods, but it is not necessary that it should be so restricted, as bought in "cheaper" lines may be helpful to create a better market. By such action a two-fold benefit is sought. One, the extent of the material damage loss is reduced compared with that of disposal otherwise of these goods and two, some trading gain may still be achieved but probably at a lower than normal level. At one time the following clause was added to a policy when requested, (usually for department stores);

"If, following damage giving rise to a claim under the policy, the Insured shall hold a salvage sale during the indemnity period, clause (a) of item No.1 of this policy shall, for the purpose of such claim, read as follows:

(a) In respect of Reduction in Turnover: the sum produced by applying the Rate of Gross Profit to the amount by which the Turnover during the indemnity, less the Turnover for the period of the salvage sale, shall in consequence of the damage, fall short of the Standard Turnover from which sum shall be deducted the Gross Profit actually earned during the period of the salvage sale."

Common sense indicates that the adjustment as provided by the clause, may need to be dealt with in two parts if the salvage sale receipts relate to a part of the business and the time period of revenue from the sale can be so divided.

With the current standard policy wording there is no need for a clause to be added to the policy to deal with either:

(a) Varying rates of gross profit by sections or
(b) Cases where a lower rate of gross profit is earned on part of the turnover for the reason of a salvage sale.

A similar aspect of the principle shown by the salvage sale adjustment can arise where after the damage, to minimise the interruption loss, production is continued but the efforts of maintaining turnover are prejudiced financially by

- [i] a higher level of waste of raw material
- [ii] different levels of quality of the products in full or part or in ratio
- [iii] a higher level of usage of materials or power etc. to achieve it.

> Thus there will be possibly no production loss itself by using a higher rate of raw materials in production or a loss of gross profit on the sale of the sub-standard goods, or combinations of these factors.

It is usually found that the adjustment to the claim can best be calculated by the method involved in the salvage sale clause.

An example is where the efficiency recovery units of a plant have themselves to cease operating by insured damage but otherwise the production continues as before. If turnover is maintained no reduction of it arises but the increased cost of operations by the reduction of efficiency is the increased usage of raw materials to maintain the production level, (if this is so), and the loss of, or gain by, the non-operation of the efficiency waste unit. The loss is an overall salvaging operation but does not easily fit in with the policy area of increased cost of working. It is however standard practice to admit payment for this type of event using the salvage sale approach to the loss calculation. This principle of allowing the consideration of the cost of action to minimise a loss to be within the policy coverage can also be seen in the provision relating to the run down of stocks as follows:

Accumulated Stocks Clause

"In adjusting any loss, account shall be taken and an equitable allowance made if any shortage in turnover due to the damage is postponed by reason of the turnover being temporarily maintained from accumulated stocks of finished goods on the insurer's premises."

This provision was advised as set out below to the insurance market in the U.K. prior to 1982 and it was stated that its ' application was a matter of market practice and thus it was not necessary for the clause to be added to policies, for it to be effective.

"Minimisation of the Loss

It is also necessary to accept that in giving attention to the policy requirement and that at common law to minimise his loss the consideration is that of the loss faced by the Insured and this is not necessarily that arising under the policy. This does not alter the policy provisions on the amount that can be recovered in the claim."

INTERRUPTION INSURANCE PRACTICAL ISSUES

3. **Outside events not arising directly from the damage but affecting the results of business.**

   These aspects need to be considered under several sub-headings as follows:

   [a] Events that arise only because of the insured damage.

   There is no inclusion in the standard U.K. Interruption Insurance policy of the word "directly" in its provisions. In generality the policy will cover such aggravation to the loss being faced, including the extension of the indemnity period (but not beyond that stated as the limit).

Examples are:

   (i) delays from public authorities etc. not granting permissions to proceed with the reinstatement work etc.
   (ii) non availability of labour, materials, etc. for such work.
   (iii) further damage (whether insured or not) to these works or replacement property in transit arising from the original insured damage and being action to minimise the loss.
   (iv) failure of preventative actions as such.
   (v) loss of customers whether by their fears that products available to them may be damaged or out of date etc, or by them to safeguard their own position whether in the result needed or not, (often a partial situation where alternative suppliers require a greater share to meet the new orders to them). What is not included is that adjustment that would have arisen in any case if no damage had occurred.

It is sometimes suggested that "customer" loss is excluded as this is not an insured peril. I do not believe that "fear" is a peril in its own right, but part of a specific event. Fear from further damage from a wall which has been impaired by an insured peril may be required to be demolished by a public authority and the loss arising is then from the original insured event [The action by the authority may need to be specific and timely and the duty for temporary reinforcement by the insured involved. These may be more associated with the material damage insurers and the property claim. The interruption loss relates to the insured acting with due diligence within common sense and an increased cost of working element can be involved].

Specific case examples are:

1. Permission of Local Council to approve the reconstruction of the works by delay in holding committee meetings to consider submitted material plans etc. all of which were in accordance with the regulations concerned. A further six months delay arose therefrom making the overall indemnity period fourteen months. The policy cover was for twelve months indemnity and this period applied.

2. Permission to reconstruct refused by the local authority despite 70% of the

property being undamaged. The Council desired to use this opportunity to re-zone the area for private dwellings only. The actual maximum indemnity period applied but the Council's efforts were partially overcome by temporary protection enabling production to continue from original site whilst insured acquired other premises and moved to them. The Local Council were unable to obtain legal support to prevent the temporary works within the policy indemnity period. The Insured was able to retain turnover to a major degree during the transfer period. The Insured bore, as his own loss, that of trading in the period outside the insured indemnity period but had a legal claim in respect of the action of the Council on the basis of the concerned "requisition of property Acts".

[b] Aspects that arise from damage to property surrounding that of the insured but not involving any damage to the insurer's own property.

The standard interruption insurance policy does not cover such loss but by an extension it can be included. It is called "Denial of Access" but this heading is somewhat misleading. The wording used is as follows:

"Property in the vicinity of the Premises, loss or destruction of or damage to which shall prevent or hinder the use of the Premises or access thereto, whether the Premises or property of the Insured therein shall be damaged or not, but excluding loss or destruction of or to any supply undertaking from which the Insured obtain electricity, gas or water, or telecommunications service which prevents or hinders the supply of such services, to the Premises."

This cover is intended to be wide enough to provide insurance under the policy from damage as insured to the internal services of electricity etc. which are common to and within other property in the vicinity. It is also not intended to exclude from the standard interruption insurance policy losses from the public etc. authorities, equipment etc. on the premises which are primarily used in the supply thereto, if damaged by an insured peril. See also page 93. The term "vicinity" may not be adequate to a particular case, and needs to be varied to meet the actual situation. It is not intended to provide adequate cover from general damage in a locality of a disastrous nature, or area damage incidents. It may however give wider cover than an underwriter anticipates in such events as the extent of cover excluded is not specified. It is not however, a general extension to Public Service Suppliers, as it so specifies.

[c] An outside event that is excluded by the policy terms.

These will be set down but the exact terms used are vital to the interpretation that applies. Generally the intention is to exclude that interruption loss flowing from the "Excepted" event. The exception may be (i) a peril (ii) a type of event - overheating etc. of electrical equipment or (iii) a class of property - explosives and each of these groups involve different considerations.

[i] a peril

If for example, war risks or nuclear event, then in general there is no insurance market as such. Special nuclear covers apply for the users of such plants, and the general "Government" view was that by excluding any defence for the consequences of such events by their operators there was no need for the ordinary business to have direct insurance for such a peril. This is, of course, not a full statement as the extent of the financial strength of the operators is not unlimited in practical terms, they are usually limited companies and the extent they can secure insurance will be subject to a policy limit, but more importantly their liability in the UK may be limited in that it excludes "indirect" liabilities as referred to at page 17.

However, when correctly drafted, the interruption policy in respect of both of these excepted perils (a) does not exclude the initial loss by an insured peril, but once the excepted peril operates and directly affects the Business, then the insured has to establish the extent of the loss from an insured peril on its own, and failure to do so results in no cover applying from the date of the event of the excepted event. This is why the nuclear event exclusion wording of the interruption policy is at variance with its counterpart in a material damage insurance policy.

Thus the effect of war conditions, is not an overall exclusion to a U.K. interruption insurance policy, unless it so stated. Engineering interruption insurance policies generally did make this an exclusion by specific terms.

An example may assist:

At a North East of England resort after the outbreak of the 1939-1945 War a cinema was damaged by a normal fire. The policy operated and the indemnity period of three years applied although the reconstruction never was possible in this period as, by wartime legislation it was not allowed as a non-essential property. However, each appropriate period of the indemnity period was adjusted to accept the level of usage that would have applied during this long period. i.e. initially cinemas were closed, afterwards the degree of usage varied with the general circumstances at that time.

The legal position can best be analysed by reference to the remarks of Slade J. in the case *Lloyd J. J. Instruments v Northern Star Insce Co.* [1987] - Although a marine insurance case it sets out the principles clearly and these were market practice in the field of interruption insurance prior to that case.

The rulings for property insurance are of long standing, see *Stanley v Western Insce. Co.* [1868] and *Pawsey v Scottish Union and National Insce. Co.* [1906], but it will be appreciated that they do not have to consider the position over a time period as arises during the indemnity period of an interruption insurance policy.

[ii] a type of event being excluded

A common exclusion under a property insurance policy is the "Electrical" clause. This is not usually added to the counterpart interruption insurance policy. Thus if, as frequently occurs, an electrical piece of apparatus overheats etc. and then there is also surrounding damage, the material damage policy will exclude the item of plant but will indemnify for the loss from the damage to surrounding property. Under the counterpart interruption policy the indemnity period is not restricted so the interruption flowing from the damage as a whole is within the cover given. It is sometimes considered that this cover will be vitiated by the material damage proviso, but this will only be so if there is no surrounding damage. The further damage will meet the proviso as worded, it does not call for total cover to apply, but it might be held depending on the facts of the extent of payment, and/or damage, under the material damage cover, i.e. it must be more than insignificant. See Section 2 for comments on the award in the case of *Glengate - K G Properties v Norwich Union* [1995]

[iii]   a class of property excluded

If the property so excluded is all that has been damaged the material damage proviso will operate to exclude cover under the interruption policy. It may also be excluded if a similar exclusion appears in the interruption insurance. However, it is not unusual for the damage to extend to include other property. There is then parallel interruption loss from the two events and it is unlikely that this loss can be separated in financial terms. The position will then turn on the extent the excluded damage loss can be held to exclude that from the insured event.

These matters have been the subject of many old law cases often in respect of marine policies. Reference is thus needed to this whole area of property insurance case law. In general, it is likely in practice that the insured will not be able to establish the actual interruption loss flowing from the insured peril unaffected by the excluded event. Failure will obviate the cover as the specified exclusion overrides the insured event in these circumstances. Without such a specified exclusion the insured event overrides the parallel loss from the unmentioned event. (*Lloyd J.J. Instruments v Northern Star Insce. Co.* [1957])

[iv]   a failure to meet a policy requirement "take all reasonable precautions / use due diligence"

It is accepted by the Courts that clauses of this nature are not to defeat the basic intention of the policy. This principle seems to have been made clear in *Fraser v Furman* [1967] but a number of individual cases exist in support. In particular in *City Tailors Ltd v Evans* [1921] L.J. Scrutton said of a clause "use due diligence" that it added nothing to the ordinary obligation of the Insured "since if the Insured failed to exercise due diligence any loss would have been caused by his own act". Reservation to the wideness of this dicta is expressed in legal works because "if the insurer's act was negligent and not wilful" it should be covered by the policy.

4. **Interruption loss aggravated by further damage to**
   (a) The insured premises disassociated with an existing loss
   (b) Premises other than the insurer's but which prejudice the existing insured loss, and only arises because of the insured event.

   Under [a] the policy operates as a fresh claim but the sum insured may be for a reduced amount, by the sum finally agreed for the first claim, unless this has been reinstated or the second loss is after the renewal date with the cover renewed. The other circumstances provision will apply to determine the level of turnover that would apply after the first loss against which the new turnover after the second loss is to be measured, and the shortfall from the second event established. Under (b) the original loss continues to be assessed. The failure by whatever cause to mitigate this loss, (provided being beyond the power of the Insured) will simply mean that this mitigation is lost and the higher loss will be admissible subject to all the conditions of the policy relating to that loss. It may mean that the Insured indemnity period is now inadequate and thus where major efforts of mitigation involve such a situation being possible, additional cover may be required to be effected to provide protection for the extended period. It is sometimes thought that such damage to other property needs to be within the perils insured, but this is not so. What has occurred is an unfortunate failure in the salvage efforts and if beyond the insurer's control, the existing cover provides for the greater loss that will arise.

   Thus, giving an extreme example of a potential aggravated loss, if a steel works supplying girders etc. for the reconstruction of the damaged property, is held back by a strike of its' workforce, or by a shortage in electricity from a Nuclear event at the supply authority's premises, the increased loss is still within the cover subject to it's otherwise provisions. Another example could be if a new replacement of plant is dropped on delivery and further time elapses before a further item can be obtained.

   This exposure to the Insurers can be mitigated by them effecting a temporary cover as appropriate.

5. **Losses arising from more than one event of which only one is insured**

   This involves a number of factors and these are dealt with at length in the Author's work "Interruption Insurance - Proximate Loss Issues".

6. **Factors which effect the Business in consequence of production or other like changes.**

   It is a rarity for a business not to be changing its' pattern of activity, either in its range of products, its updating of its production methods or the plant it uses, or entering or exiting from geographical areas or manner in which it conducts its sales, within an annual frequency time. Thus the basic principle of the UK interruption formula of indemnity based on the corresponding previous time period's result compared with those post the insured event, brings into play how appropriate adjustments can be made to endeavour to provide realism to the loss adjustment that will be given. This matter is dealt with by the "other circumstances" provision, but it must be realised that the adjustments will need careful consideration of that which would have taken place without the insured damage having occurred.

It is therefore important to consider how to approach the obtaining of the information so involved. A general review of the business and its activities will initially provide the nature of a practical review. Thus an hotel will normally show little change unless it is pre-publicised, or recorded. In the cases of industry, this predecision making will often be in ten stages:

- [i] the pre-research
- [ii] the planning documents and boardroom approvals
- [iii] the financial borrowing agreements
- [iv] pre-sales forecasts and customer relationships
- [v] the construction work and plant delivery times and methods
- [vi] the engagement of employees, often over a period and by categories.
- [vii] the purchase agreements of production materials and delivery dates and quantities
- [viii] preliminary production runs and quality etc. testing
- [ix] scheduled delivery dates to customers and build up of quantities including own stock holding levels and
- [x] the degree of margin to each stage allowed to be practical.

In the event of damage to property involved or at any suppliers premises included in the cover, and bearing in mind the data disclosed when the insurance was placed, (if it was on an "Advance Interruption" basis, the financial exposure from "a date when" aspect) are capable of analysis and assessment against the time when revenue would arise, its extent and build-up, the savings possible from delays, the efforts to minimise the loss and their worth, and then established on a practical level. For a partial change in a business the same considerations, or some of them, will also apply.

The matter may involve a modified product or a newer model and then the question of the practical steps to minimise the loss will call for a commercial judgement. What must not be overlooked is the problem of [i] the factor commercially of continuing sales of a sub-standard or dated model or loss of market of the new one when it finally becomes available [ii] the aspect of spares and the continued market of them against that which would have happened. The loss in value of undamaged stock arising is not protected by the interruption policy, it is a capital asset and can be insured as such by a material damage policy. It can be a legitimate item in full or part of the increased cost of working claim, although it needs to give rise to the advantage resulting within the maximum indemnity period, and the extent arising from the insured damage; and outside the pure loss in the value of the stock asset.

7. Government, Public or other Authority regulations or Tax changes etc.

The initial aspect to be considered is when the changes would have been brought into force, and if the damage itself has been implemental in the change being made to apply. The basic rule is as indicated under (3) above, i.e. It is the comparison with the "would have been" situation that is all important and, unless specifically excluded, the indirect or other events that then come into play are not excluded events from the standard interruption insurance policy.

The problem can arise for example re import or export charges or even permission for it to be adopted. Thus switching imports to meet production demands, through limitations of local supplies or use of another country to meet the needs, if agreed to minimise the loss, will be part of these costs, subject to the policy's other provisions. In a similar way changes in export markets can give rise to a variation in costs to the business.

A further problem will arise where the property damage loss involves foreign machinery etc. The extent of the material damage insurance cover may not have been arranged to include the costs of import taxes or the policy may be otherwise inadequate. If by specially importing to mitigate the interruption loss otherwise arising then consideration of the amount does arise as a matter of increased costs of working.

However, there are further points to review:

[i] the inadequacy of the property cover which falls only under the material damage policy which is excluded as arising from that reason and not from the damage itself.
[ii] any gain in value permanently by the replacement, a residual value assessment
[iii] the aspect of the depreciation or other tax allowances than can arise
[iv] any reduction, or gain, in the practical usage or output of the new plant etc. This may be a matter of the production machinery as a whole where new modern plant may involve less separate equipment etc.

In chemical or petrochemical companies the changes in size, methods, standards of product grades from plant, demand changes, decisions to continue production against the capital usage in the future, are not uncommon and the insured event brings into play an earlier review of the matter. Fundamentally the basic principle will be to create a maximum sum of the indemnity under the policy, if a normal recovery was undertaken, bearing in mind policy limitations of average, indemnity period etc., and for the variations to be mutually agreed as a method of minimising the loss by reducing the amount payable under the contract suitably.

Examples in this area are:

[a] The replacement of a 100,000 ton capacity plant by one of 350,000 tons and the extra to be (partially designed) to feed a new plant project introduced by the need for the economic rebuilding of the destroyed former facility.

[b] Serious damage occurring to a retail shop selling bridal gowns etc.

In the centre of a city the area was designated for closure at a date within the maximum indemnity period, but in fact the programme of road development was running some months in arrears. The factual situation was that originally the date of closure of the shop, if it had been met, would have, in practical terms, have ended the indemnity period to apply. However, the fact was that trading would, therefore be continued for a longer period. Thus the practical date of the end of the indemnity period was extended but not longer than the maximum insured by the policy. However, the effect of this extension was to reduce the efforts involved in running the business against the unavoidable closure date, even if somewhat unknown. Therefore it was necessary to have regard to the level of turnover that could be expected in the extended period. By the factual closure in the circumstances the level of the continuing overheads of the business need to be reviewed, advertising, wages, etc. and how the level of stock which, being of a specialist nature, would have been adjusted in this closing down period and the effect that would have had on the business results in any case.

In another example, the interruption was able to be minimised by importing a base intermediate material, but this resulted in the tax authorities requiring this higher level of imports to carry a surcharge import cost. Reference to those authorities obtained some relief but a higher charge still subsisted which became part of the increased cost of working claim.

See also page 16 (final paragraph).

8. Weather or holiday period considerations

It is surprising to find the number of business firms that are affected by factors related to the time of the year. Where short indemnity periods apply following damage, the comparative aspect of the loss calculation formula will require detailed and careful review to ensure that the resultant data does produce the correct figures.

Hotels during the winter season may be shut, or if open, involve exceptional Christmas trade but otherwise until Spring give discounts to attract guests. The use of a Net Revenue type wording [Revenue being defined as income less cost of food drink and tobacco products] simplifies the loss calculation but the comparisons involved must equate the specific date periods and sometimes the general weather applying.

Departmental Stores and many retail shops have wide variations in the day-to-day turnover often associated with seasonal holidays, Easter etc. with regard to birthday cards etc. and Mothers/Fathers day events and trade at the beginning of school terms, as well as the fashion factors at Spring and Autumn. It needs to be remembered that the prior ordering will give a vital clue to the turnover possibilities and the problem of late replacement if such stocks are damaged or destroyed.

Colleges and schools, especially if boarding is involved, have the complication of payment by terms but expecting a yearly or longer period of income from scholars. The damage to part of the premises may prejudice the whole or unequal part of the revenue and the costs, and some non-standing charges, may not fall away *pro rata* in the actual event. It is essential to pre-plan the cover to meet the need in whatever manner it arises.

Travel related businesses and major sporting or like events, whether one off or not, are also typical. There are cases where planning is needed and disclosure to avoid the over reliance on the comparative basis of the policy indemnity formula and difficulties at the time of a claim. The shortfall of a settlement may involve inadequate advice from the broker or adviser to the insured. A pre-review of the nature and timing of revenue of the business will usually enable a check to be made of these factors, the needed adjustments made and clarity of the settlement process agreed with the insurer, at the time the insurance is being arranged.

A special review will also be needed where a business [aircraft manufacturers, ship-builders, specialist machinery, such as printing presses etc.] has its income spread over more than an annual time basis. Although payments on account will normally be involved these will usually be after a retained sum and the timing at pre-agreed dates. They are not necessarily indicative of the actual effort of the business nor variation to them a guide to the financial loss of trading being suffered by the business. Delay to the scheduled delivery date of this type of property may also involve loss of its sale and also loss of associated further deliveries and revenue therefrom. The solution of adopting a longer insured indemnity period may not provide for the full financial loss that can arise. The cancellation of follow up orders involves consideration of the major changes that can arise, including the retention or otherwise of the skilled labour force, and the ability to find new customers in the specialist area involved. The knock-on situation will also need to be considered, re suppliers, not only re the extension to the main organisation's insurance but also for the separate insurances of those suppliers. It will involve both the material loss of assets already made, those to be made or work to be completed as well as the trading interruption that will arise. The underwriter in such cases can face a very high percentage loss ratio and very low possibilities for reduction of it by salvage type operations.

9. Lack of finance or ability to recover from the damage

This area of events can produce a number of problems:

[i] lack of finance to rebuild or repair etc. It is the insured's task to minimise his loss and the inadequacy of the material damage insurance is basically outside the interruption insurance contract. It is not considered that this can be over ridden

by the argument that the problem would not have arisen but for the insured event. The material damage proviso deals with total non-insurance by the insured of that for which he would normally effect cover. See page 25.

However, where the material damage proviso has not been breached, (under insurance or outside responsibility to insure applies) the consequence of delays in or non-replacement of the damaged property outside the control of the insured may involve the actual indemnity period, being longer. The policy cover will include this lengthier period up to the maximum limit by the policy terms.

Examples are:
- [i] delays arising from outside bodies (such as public authorities) being slow in granting necessary approvals.
- [ii] landlords wishing to develop or repair in a different way or extent or wishing to prevent return of a tenant or lessee.
- [iii] property owned by small Trusts or individuals who have inadequate funds to deal with under insurance by giving rise to lack of finance.

See also page 14.

The recovery rights against such persons or authorities by the insured (and hence the insurers) are extremely limited. The English Law of TORT excludes consequential loss except directly arising from the physical damage. The legal principle is *"dannum sine injuria"* and the following cases outline the points involved:

Brandon Electrical Engineering Co v William Press & Sons [1956]
Dalziel of (Airdrie) Ltd v The Burgh of Airdrie [1966]
Elliott v Sir Robert McAlpine & Sons Ltd [1966]
Electrochrome v Welsh Plastics Ltd [1968]
British Celanese Ltd v A. H. Hunt (Capacitors) Ltd [1969]
S.C.M. (United Kingdom) Ltd. v W.J. Whittall & Sons Ltd
[16.7.70 Court of Appeal].

The rights of the insurer are limited to those of the insured, but if subrogation action is taken (thus by the insured) it must be for the full total loss that he has suffered. i.e. including any deductible or reduction in consequence of under insurance.

Overseas the strictness of this legal ruling may be reduced, as evidenced in a case in Australia relative to the consequential loss by the cutting of a pipeline by a ship in Botany Bay harbour where it was considered that the knowledge of it should have been clear to the ships' master and thus liable for not only the damage, but the consequential loss arising from the loss of oil to the third party concerned. *Caltex Oil (Australia) Pty. Ltd v The Dredge "Willemsted"*, (1977).

It is not unusual for insurers to waive subrogation rights of recovery by a clause in the policy in respect of associated or subsidiary companies forming an overall conglomerate.

10. Other miscellaneous items

(a) Payments on account

It is normal practice in respect of the adjustment of insurance claims in the United Kingdom under material damage and interruption policies for payments on account to be made after the event pending the final settlement which may well be months later. Sometimes a policy clause sets down that these may be made.

Insurance policies are contracts of "good faith" and the prompt settlement of claims is within the intentions of the parties and the clause does not alter the basic position. In an interruption policy the normal Condition 4 envisages that over-payment may arise and that return of such a sum is required.

The non-payment of the estimated loss to a later date is not complying with the cover granted by insurance and it can prejudice the position by delaying reconstruction or repair etc. and recovery of the trading and turnover. Thus payments on account assist the insurers as well as the insured. Non-payment may arise because the claim is rejected or the cover disputed. A Court decision will determine disputes but if successful an insured may well receive not only the costs of the action but interest on the amount due in settlement. Thus if undue delay arises interest may be a legitimate part of the amount that an insured should receive.

In general, the precise extent of the material damage and interruption loss to a date may well be an estimate only, nevertheless it is usually possible to have a reasonable idea of the financial strain on the business at stated times after the insured event. Usually payments on account, even if within a safety margin, are made by agreement, against such assessments.

The material damage payments are due as indemnity in amount immediately after the event, and it will only be the additional sums, such as "new for old" or similar policy provisions, that need to be withheld until spent thereto by the insured. There is no case for a Loss Adjuster to suggest that payments on account for material damage cover are totally non payable until the costs have arisen and been paid by the insured. If builders are paid by installment as the work proceeds there may be early recovery by the insured under this heading of claim to some extent. This may well compensate for the fact that the interruption policy payments by their nature will be somewhat in arrears of the cash strain being met. For example, continued unearned by activity remuneration of employees retained and within the interruption policy cover, arise weekly or monthly and it may well be that to this extent payments on account under this policy need to be made.

As the indemnity period continues it is usual to find that the degree of accuracy of estimates will be greater and the periodic payments adjusted accordingly.

Sometimes the "payments on account" clause is worded to state that they will be made. Non payment then may well be a breach of the policy provision with the Insurers being liable for any financial loss resulting therefrom. It is, of course, necessary in all such cases for the Insured to have submitted his claim with the necessary supporting data.

(b) Residual value.

This term relates to that part of the increased costs of working which in the event will be in respect of [a] existing value after the indemnity period insured has been concluded, [b] continuing to be of value to the business, and/or [c] required by the insured to remain and not only for the cost of making good falling under the claim itself. As they have been included in the claim figures to this extent the ownership lies with the insurers. It is sometimes argued that the policy makes no reference to such a matter but the principle lies within the terms of the indemnity provided by item 1[b] "increase in cost of working." This wording is usually:

"The additional expenditure necessarily and reasonably incurred for the sole purpose of avoiding or diminishing the reduction in turnover which but for that expenditure would have taken place during the Indemnity Period in consequence of the incident, but not exceeding the sum produced by applying the Rate of Gross Profit to the amount of the reduction thereby avoided."

The actual adjustment is a matter for mutual agreement by the parties, i.e. the value of the property concerned to the business for the future operations against the value to be obtained by its' removal after the cost of making good.

Expenditure that falls for consideration as increased in cost of working may include items such as:

(i) capital items - temporary plant hired or bought, temporary lighting other electrical or other services or rearrangement expenses etc.
(ii) semi capital/running costs - rent of external premises or property additional to that normally applying
(iii) standing or temporary charges - additional security costs [extra guards, lighting or patrol visits etc.] but that part of such costs which relate to the benefit of the material damage insurers must be allocated to them.
(iv) salvage sale type costs, if any, after the proper allocation of these to the stock insurers. See also page 6.
(v) special emergency costs such as buying another business, hiring production from elsewhere, or buying completed products to maintain customers.

Over emphasis is not to be given to the word "sole". It does not mean that any expenditure that has other benefits, to that of reducing the interruption claim, are not insured at all. In such cases it is that part, that gives the benefit, that is within the terms of the cover. If a benefit which has no "residual" value has a benefit value longer than that of the actual indemnity period involved, it is not normal for any adjustment to be claimed for this. It would be needed for the insurers to establish the amount of this precisely and failure to establish the amount would result in no adjustment being allowable at law.

There is not any legal principle [as exists under Marine insurance] of "General Average" with the parties who benefit from salvage costs having to contribute to them in proportion to their interests.

(c) Misunderstandings re "Savings" and effect of increased turnover on the "Rate of Gross Profit."

The interruption policy relates to loss as set down as a whole. It does not relate to each standing charge and profit or loss of a business separately. This is particularly seen when the "Gross Profit" definition is defined on the difference basis, but it applies equally on covers using other definitions of "Gross Profit".

The principle incorporates the fact that if "turnover" and the "non-insured charges" are both constant elements as they should be, as 100% represents turnover and non-insured charges is intended to be the sum of "variable" charges, i.e. those that vary directly with turnover, then the resultant reduction of one from the other will give a constant ratio.

It is this factor that is the reason why, theoretically, daily changes of the items within the "Gross Profit" definition are not important as the sum of them is constant and the policy cover relates to them as a whole. It follows that the question of when payments for overheads are made against what time period of them are involved can be disregarded as it is the final overall yearly figures that will produce the correct "Rate of Gross Profit" "that will be needed and used. In effect the balance of the sum of the insured element of business charges are dealt with by a corresponding change in the profit or loss [trading] factor.

Thus, if turnover increases or reduces, the constant factor of the "Rate of Gross Profit" will not be changed thereby. The internal elements of the insured "Gross Profit" may change, but self-balance with the profit or loss allocation.

A change to the Rate of Gross Profit can arise irrespective of the level of turnover and will be because the sum of the "Non-insured charges" has changed upwards or downwards from the previous level, as a ratio.

However, an increase in turnover indicates that without any other factor the level of individual insured charges will either vary directly or will result in the adjustment to the trading profit or loss directly. If any actual insured charge would change in the period of the business involved within the insured indemnity period and a claim is being made, then the actual level of each insured charge that would apply, needs to be considered against the 'would have been' level to establish the "savings" of the business that should be deducted from the figure obtained by the application of the rate of gross profit to the reduction in turnover involved. Otherwise, that rate will provide the sum of the increase in level of a charge, that in fact will not have to be borne.

(d)   Interest payable and matters that can arise therefrom.

An issue sometimes arises regarding the interest payable by a business in its trading activities, such as bank loans, hire purchase repayments etc. and the counterpart aspect of interest that may be earned on the receipts from the material damage claim prior to those costs being incurred. Briefly the interruption insurance policy involves the definition of Gross Profit which will include within its scope the standing charges of the business and one of these will be the costs of finance used in the business additional to its capital, whether private or shareholders funds etc. When there is a reduction in turnover then the contribution to Gross Profit is the basis of the indemnity formula, this provides for the continued relative cost of financing the business (loan etc. interest or shareholders dividends). In actual fact the effect of the interruption can be to increase the amount of the finance borrowings to meet the costs which in due course will be repaid by the insurance payments. The cash flow problems caused by the gap, between payments of these costs and receipts from the insurers, will need to be met. However, by payments on account and the rebuilding costs etc. not being payable by the insured immediately, this cash flow gap could, in theory, be adverse or favourable to the business. Any shortfall avoidly rising from under insurance is to be excluded in this consideration, as it arises outside the scope of either policy.

Generally insurers are adverse to considering any of the cash flow strain [increased by the damage] as being within the policy cover. This is not fully correct, as for example the interest charges on borrowings that fall under the heading of Increased Costs, until payment is made for these, is a legitimate part of the increased costs claim. The other part of such costs from the later settlement of the interruption insurance formula claim is, in my view, only admissible for undue delay in either payments on account [the policy Claims Condition 1(c) indicates the normality of such a payment and it is normal for a policy condition to provide for them], or the loss settlement itself [as under the principle of "good faith" this is an essential part of the indemnity offered by the insurers.]

The payment of the material damage loss is in itself a separate issue and the previous reference to it mitigating the cash flow loss may not be strictly correct. Two issues arise:

(i)   The material damage policy is a separate contract, unless it is a combined policy [see (ii) below] and the indemnity payable thereunder is a separate matter standing on the terms of that contract. Thus payments on account are normal, stock claims can be dealt with on their own, some part of the indemnity may, by its nature and policy condition, be deferred [reinstatement covers]. The payment is not tied to the continuation of the business etc. and other parties not involved with the interruption insurance may have policy interests which call for the loss settlement not to be delayed.

(ii) If a combined policy applies then the actual sub-division between the sectional classes of cover and the provision for claim payments need to be considered. Probably as a single overall contract it may be that if settlement is disputed or delayed payments only are made;, the overall effect on meeting their liability will be the determining factor on any nterest that will arise for inclusion in a disputed settlement.

(e) Policy cover relative to employees and their rights.

The rights of employees themselves under the contract has not been the subject of any U.K. court action. A number of aspects arise including the right to take benefit from a contract allegedly effected on their behalf. It may be indicative of the modern outlook to quote a German court decision [reference unknown] which upheld the workers claim for unfair dismissal following insured damage on the grounds that it arose not from the damage but from the lack of insurance on wages.

(f) So called Consequential Losses and from whence indemnity normally lies.

Damage to property may frequently result in remote loss, at law referred to as a consequential loss, hence the advantage of not using that term but to refer to interruption insurance as the class of insurance involved. For example, [i] the cost of rebuilding may be increased because of the delay to its start compared with that planned, or from the date of the actual damage when liability under a material damage insurance policy will be calculated unless otherwise provided. [ii] the interest on borrowed capital for a new project, or less often, on the cost of rebuilding after damage through late indemnity payment.

None of these costs, which are of a capital nature, are included within a standard interruption insurance policy, but a special cover has, on rare occasions, been offered by the C.L. Dept to provide for the continuing extra interest cost to the extent it can be established. (that is outside such costs that can derive from agreed costs under the Increase in cost of working provisions of the gross profit item of the interruption policy).

(C) SUMMARY AND CONCLUSION

Thus, at this stage, a summary can be made of the financial aspects of the claim in accordance with the policy formula i.e. the reduction in turnover, the increased costs of working, which will be factual and need to be established in accordance with the policy wording, the individual adjustments sought under the provisions thereto, each with supporting comment and evidence as far as possible and savings of expenditure that falls under the headings of charges included within the definition of "Gross Profit." Then, reduction of this total sum by the provisions of the policy, if under insurance provisions apply.

If the remuneration of employees, (to the extent these are defined), are insured by a separate item, then the calculation of the claim thereunder will follow the same principles as those stated in regard to the "Gross Profit" item, but will be subject to the limits etc. that are incorporated in this separate item of cover.

The wording of the policy with regard to under insurance, if not on a "declaration" basis, relates to the "would have been" level for the twelve months (multiplied by the appropriate factor if the indemnity period exceeds twelve months). The actual indemnity period applicable is not that to be used and if this should be less than twelve months the comparison is still to be in respect of annual figures. Thus any "trend etc." operating after twelve months from the date of the damage is not relevant to this adjustment.

THE CLAIM CALCULATION DETAILS NEED TO BE SET DOWN FIRSTLY WITHOUT THE ADJUSTMENT FACTORS AND THEN FOR THESE TO BE INDIVIDUALLY STATED WITH THE MONETARY RESULT ARISING FROM EACH.

By such clear submission of data, the onus is then on the insurer to submit his case if he seeks to vary them or wishes to submit others that he considers relevant. Both parties are frequently surprised as for example seeking a higher "trend" factor may initially increase the amount involved but the final adjustment, if under insurance is applicable, may result in no increase in the overall figure otherwise arising. Extending the indemnity period claimed may introduce problems regarding the adjustments under the "trend" provision as the data may not be applicable evenly over an extended period.

Trend as a whole is an amalgam of:
- production level and customer availability
- price and inflation factors against competition
- falling demand of older products against new products and the sale prospects for them.
- success in market penetration against other producers etc.

as well as consideration of the overall factors of area, economic, social, fashion etc. that are to be met in today's world. For example, tobacco sales are not only affected directly but associated products such as lighters, ashtrays etc. will be affected by tax and health etc. legislation.

Thus, the longer the indemnity claimed and within the policy cover, the more difficult it is to assess the "trend" factor and a simple adjustment with only clear data adjustments may allow the expedition of the settlement to be commercially preferable.

SECTION 2

THE APPLICATION OF THE "MATERIAL DAMAGE" PROVISION

"If a detailed, semantic and syntactical analysis of words in a commercial contract led to a conclusion that flouted business common sense, then they had to be made to yield to business common sense." Lord Diplock in "The Antaios".

Introductory remarks

The use of the material damage requirement has been a feature of U.K. interruption insurance policies virtually from the inception of this class of cover in the early twentieth century. It is however, not usually found in engineering breakdown of machinery and the like interruption insurances which date from sometime later and present different needs of control of this aspect.

The wording has not changed over the period excepting the addition of proviso [ii]. It reads, and is usually found on the face of the policy after the setting out of the contract terms.

"...the Insurer will pay to the Insured.......loss resulting from such interruption or interference provided that:

at the same time of the happening of the loss destruction or damage there shall be in force an insurance covering the interest of the Insured in the property at the Premises against such destruction or damage and that

>   [i]   *payment shall have been made or liability admitted therefor, or*
>   [ii] *payment would have been made or liability admitted therefor but for the operation of a proviso in such insurance excluding liability for losses below a specified amount."*

Its intention has always been made clear i.e. to make the control provisions, warranties, description, requirements etc. of the counterpart material damage policy to be incorporated into the associated interruption insurance contract without the need to specifically repeat them in that document. Additionally it is to make some effort to see that there will be funds available to provide for the repair or reinstatement of the physical damage suffered.

It is by no means uncommon for the interruption cover to be placed with one insurer and the material damage insurance contract to be with another. So to associate the contracts simplifies the transaction of the interruption placement and provides, in part, for the changes which can take place resulting in amendment of the material damage insurance terms etc. following alterations in the hazards of the property concerned. It also assists in the handling of investigations that follow a loss, by allowing much of these to be left with those dealing with the material damage claim settlement.

Some historical notes.

Prior to 1939 when the basic current interruption U.K. policy cover was introduced, its policy terms provided as follows:

> [i] the premises or property therein of the insured shall be destroyed or damaged by fire, and
>
> [ii] the business shall be thereby interrupted or interfered with."

The post 1939 policy counterpart clausing is as follows:

"any building or other property or any part thereof used by the Insured at the Premises for the purpose of the Business".

Thus, there is now no reference to ownership of the property by the Insured.

In 1947 Mr. E.L. Butler F.C.I.I., a recognised authority, was the author of a booklet setting down the changes arising from the new post 1939 policy form and this was accepted as providing an official view of the matter. The work made the following remarks relative to the "material damage" provision:

"This proviso does not apply to all the property comprised in the descriptions set out in lines 6 and 7 [i.e. any Insured at the Premises for the purpose of the Business..] but only to the interest of the Insured in the property at the Premises. The Premises occupied by the Insured may be held on a lease containing a covenant by the lessors that they will take out and maintain an insurance against fire. In these circumstances the maintenance of the insurance is not a matter within the control of the Insured, and it would be unreasonable to expect him to take out an additional insurance in his own name. Similar conditions may apply to machinery or other property used by the Insured but owned by others. The provision, therefore, is only concerned with property in which the Insured has an interest and which he can reasonably be expected to insure."

General Market Understanding

It has always been the practice of major U K insurers to treat the material damage provision as applying to the Insured having to effect insurances against the perils that the interruption insurance is to provide indemnity, insofar as it is normal and usual for that Insured to effect such cover. i.e. where by lease the responsibility for insurance of the premises lie with the landlord it is not reasonable to require the policy holder of the interruption insurance to additionally effect material damage insurance to ensure that the provision has been met. This position might not be fully accepted if the lease provisions are limited to certain perils only and the interruption insurance effected by the lessee for his business includes a further range of perils. To ensure that the material damage provision is met in such cases it will be necessary for either:

- [a] The additional peril cover to be arranged by the lessee

or

- [b] The lease requirements in the event of damage by such further perils to be the responsibility of the landlord.

The non affecting of insurance by a landlord in such circumstances, which may well be the case for all perils where the landlord is a public authority or corporation which carries its own insurance cover, is to relieve the lessee from having to meet the material damage provision and to leave his interruption insurance otherwise to be fully effective. The same position would obtain if by the use of a deductible, the property policy of the landlord did not provide for payment.

The material damage provision also is not applicable to interruption policy extensions re suppliers, customers, sub-contractors and the like.

This matter was one of the items in dispute in the case - *Glengate-KG Properties v Norwich Union Fire & Others* [1957] and Appeal [1957]

At first instance Judge Phillips J. indicated:

[a] That against a material damage cover for £15 million, the non insurance to a minor degree of plans as such would not be a breach

[b] The material damage proviso was met and was not to be subdivided in application.

It might not have been raised as an issue if the full facts at disclosure had been circulated (the matter was dealt with in separate sections giving rise to this point re the material damage proviso not being clarified earlier). There was an office contents insurance in force for the Plaintiff in respect of their offices at another address and this, it is thought, had the usual extension clause re plans etc. being protected up to a limit whilst elsewhere.

At the Court of Appeal the majority of two Judges ruled that the material damage provision had been met but the dissenting Judge considered that the matter should be decided using the criteria that a person has a right to insure that which, if damaged or destroyed, would give rise to a financial loss to him and he should so act. Such a decision would cause many difficulties. For example, would it be necessary for a shopkeeper to insure the pavements outside his premises or for a garage proprietor to insure the hardstandings on which cars are parked to secure the effective operation of his interruption insurance? The ruling makes clear that the initial view expressed by Mr. Butler (reasonably expected) does apply, and it also may indicate that while a substantial cover may allow no breach by a minor area of non insured property, an insignificant material damage insurance will not be deemed to be adequate to meet the proviso.

SECTION 3

THE MEANING OF THE TERM "PREMISES"

"When I use a word, "Humpty Dumpty said in a rather scornful tone, it means just what I choose it to mean", - neither more nor less."
  - Lewis Carroll

However, the word 'premises' "includes the land and all buildings and appurtenances within an enclosed space at the location specified." -
"Principles and Practice of Interruption Insurance" by Hickmott

A legal definition of "premises" has stated "land and buildings upon it".

The standard U K policy wording in its "preamble" sets down the following:

"that if....any building or other property or any part thereof used by the Insured at the Premises for the purpose of the Business be destroyed or damaged by..."

It is therefore appropriate to analyse this paragraph in detail.

[i] "any part thereof" has been taken in the U K interruption insurance market to mean to include land, outside concrete or other hardstandings and the services to the property whether under or over ground and in broad terms, anything of this nature on which the business depends. Thus covers relating to garages and transport parks include under this preamble such outside matters. This does not override the subsequent requirements of the policy.

[ii] "used by the Insured." A broad interpretation of this term has been adopted by the insurance market and in the negotiations in arranging an insurance the nature of the association of the Insured to the property, the subject of the cover, is usually apparent or the insurer does not seek any further knowledge from that indicated in these discussions.

In the case of *Glengate K G v Norwich Union and Others* [1995] at the initial Court hearing Phillips, J. indicated his support for this, the interruption insurance being in the form of an "Advance Rent" cover by a property developer in respect of a property acquired by them whilst it was being redeveloped for future occupation by letting.

It also involves the market acceptance of public utility or like plants or apparatus on a site of the Insured where the use of them is basically for the supply of the service to the Insured. If brought onto the site so also would cranes and the like. Under the normal contract conditions, the responsibility for them is borne by the hirer and the contract often includes the provision of the specialist operator but the degree to which the hirer assumes control of such may not be clear.

[iii] "at the premises." While this may seem a simple phrase, care is necessary in some cases to make clear the extent of this provision. Multi-tenanted property, shopping malls, shops within shops etc. need to specify the extent of the term "premises."

However, in a letter to the British Insurance Brokers Association of August 1980, the then Fire Offices Committee, confirmed that irrespective of the narrowness of the "premises" definition of a policy, Offices would generally adopt a more liberal interpretation by regarding damage to an area of "common access and usage" in multi-tenure and precinct type buildings as capable of initiating a loss under a C. L. policy, (a reference to the older term for an interruption insurance policy). The areas which we have in mind would be common entrances, corridors, walkways, staircases, lifts, roofs, services (lighting, heating, power, water, sanitation etc) car parks and the like. You will appreciate that it is difficult to be exhaustive on this subject or give other than general guidelines. In fact to be too specific would be detrimental to the Insured, since this could inhibit the freedom of Offices to settle losses in accordance with their individual merits.

It will be seen that by this letter's reference to car parks, more than "buildings" has always been contemplated as being in the scope of the term "premises" and this is discussed further later.

The matter also has to be considered in the light of the "material damage proviso" as discussed in the preceding Section 2.

It will be seen that the word "premises" will be the subject in each policy with added details relevant to it, and that the preceding words "any buildings.. part thereof.." need to be considered together. Thus the market practice of including land etc, as set out above, makes for the commercial sense needed to provide adequate cover for the many situations that are involved without lengthy and complex clausing having to be adopted. The underwriter should be fully aware of the nature of the physical situation to be expected in the various trades and industries which will be the subject of interruption insurance proposed to him. He will in the larger cases, normally have an insurance report by a specialist in that area.

Where underground workings are involved special care is needed by the underwriter to clarify the extent of his cover. It is usually to exclude this operation of the business completely but this needs to be stated specifically to be effective. It is not safe to rely on the material damage provision as machinery may be insured on a blanket basis and then will be insured, intentionally or otherwise, whilst underground and damage to it meets this provision. See additional comments in Section 2.

Subsidiary plants are not uncommon today and their ownership is frequently held by the contract supplier involved, although on the land at the premises. By market agreement in the 1980's it was agreed to accept such plants as within the scope of the interruption insurance of the main business provided they were dedicated to the supply of the business thereat. The gross profit etc. of the supply operator is not included and needs a separate policy with the extension of cover to the main business set down specifically.

In respect of certain perils, care is also needed to appreciate the cover applying. For example "flood" is usually involving an area additional to the insured premises. Thus it is necessary to establish that damage occurred at the premises itself, not just that the flood waters prevented access, or the operation of the plant. This does not of itself constitute damage unless an "All Risks" form of cover applies when the exclusion provisions will be involved. These exclusion provisions have to be considered firstly in regard to the material damage cover and then the interruption insurance cover itself, secondly how each on its own provides protection and then has the material damage provision been met by admission thereunder of some damage. For example, damage to a transformer may be excluded by the material damage policy by specific inclusion of an electrical exclusion clause, but this not appearing on the interruption policy will mean that damage from this incident is not excluded. If the damage is beyond the actual machine then the material damage policy may provide for some payment and in turn enable the whole interruption loss to be payable.

Originally some insurers included an electrical exclusion proviso in their standard interruption insurance form, but this practice seems to have fallen into disuse. It has also to be remembered that this type of incident can bring into issue the degree of loss arising from the two events and without specific clausing the loss flowing from both may initially be within the cover and the task of quantifying that from the uninsured event falls on the insurer, with the full loss being payable if it fails to establish this.

A complex situation can arise where the operation of the business involves open cast mining, quarrying or the like. The effect of flooding can give rise to a very serious interruption to the activities of the business, but [i] what property that has been damaged has been insured? And [ii] what interruption overall has arisen? Damage to the overground machinery, such as huge draglines etc, may be minimal or serious and the residual value of the workings maintained, (but over what length of time?) and the adjustment of the amortisation factor difficult to agree.

The rising of a river level may prevent the continuation of the disposal of effluent by the mere closure of the discharge pipe back-flow valve, resulting in cessation of production. This loss is not covered but on whom lies the fault of non advice?

Problems from area damage may also arise in respect of insurances including the perils of explosion, aircraft disasters, storms or tempest etc., and disastrous fires in poorly constructed or congested areas of cities etc. and the extent of the insurance protection intended by the Underwriter will be determined by the policy terms and not his or the insureds' wishes or hopes. The policy will be interpreted as any contract against the preparer of it [usually the insurer] unless there are clear grounds to challenge the meaning of the wording set down.

A case is on record of a huge geographical area in Africa which had not been the subject of other than modest rainfall for many tens of years being suddenly subjected to abnormal rain resulting in a major part of it being flooded to a significant depth of water. Part of the huge area was in fact a large salt pan and by pipes and pumps this product was recovered for despatch elsewhere on that Continent to maintain the

Insureds' chemical plant activities. There was material damage insurance on the pipes, pumps etc. and payment thereunder agreed. The interruption loss was, not only the salt pan site, but that from downstream activities and was for a major sum. An overall policy applied and the only challenge that could be made was regarding the fact that the raw salt itself was not insured. It was considered that this was not a requirement under the interruption cover and damage to plant by an insured peril having occurred and a material loss payment also [so that the material loss provision had been met] the whole loss was recoverable under the policy subject to deductible and average etc. provisions. The loss was in effect flowing from the damage to the insured property and the parallel loss of inability to work this equipment and operate on the site did not exclude the loss arising within the insured indemnity period.

See Section 1 [d] also for the considerations that need to be considered.

SECTION 4

THE APPLICATION OF NON DISCLOSURE

"But now, gentlemen, there is another innovation, extension, or development, evolved by the ingenuity of a few actuaries following the unscientific daring of Lloyd's. I mean profit policies - insurances against loss of profit. This, of course, is a more definite infringement of the principle of indemnity because as you give a man SOMETHING HE NEVER HAD, you can hardly be said to be recouping him of the loss that which he once possessed."

... "Everything can be defended, or where would the lawyers be?.. Are they calculated to mitigate loss or lessen misfortune without injuring society in general? To put it plainly, are they not likely to make rogues of honest men?" - Excerpts from an address by Mr S.J. Pipkin in Glasgow 1905.

The House of Lords in the case of Pan Atlantic v Pine Top [1994] restated the legal principle applicable and this is therefore current decided law. Parts of the rulings under C.T.I. v Oceanus [1984] were overruled.

A. GENERAL

The following heads indicate the matters to be considered by the Court to reach a decision:

1. Was the fact or circumstance alleged to have been misrepresented or not disclosed "material", in the sense that a prudent insurer would have wanted the full and true position to take it into account in deciding whether, and if so, on what terms it would underwrite the case. [The word "prudent" is, I believe, still used in the original sense as in many former law decisions, that of an experienced underwriter in the market of the relevant class of insurance - a practical person- and not a careful person who avoids danger in any form if at all possible - which is not, of course, the insurance function.]

2. Has the requirement in the actual case been waived

3. Has the right to avoid been lost by some legal bar

4. Has the actual misrepresentation or non-disclosure induced the particular insurer to write the business on the terms set down.

If "materiality" under [1] is established then "inducement" under [4] will be presumed and the onus will lie on the Insured to prove that, with the true position known to the insurer at the time of the placing of the cover they would probably have written the business on the terms that applied.

In practice, it is likely that the insurer will be faced with the following:

(a) What induced them initially to write the case and from what aspect(s) arising from the full disclosure are there grounds for their view that they would have declined the business or imposed harsher terms.

(b) Disclosure of their current, at the time, underwriting files and rules that are relevant
(c) Details of insurance cases that are similar and the terms etc. applied to them as shown in their books.

The former practice of calling an outside " insurance expert" for his views may fall into disuse as the past experience from them of convenient hindsight has down-graded the weight of their submissions.

B. LEGAL PRINCIPLES INVOLVED

The duty of disclosure arises from the general principle of *"Uberrima fides"* or in English - utmost good faith. As was said in an early Court case *"As the underwriter knows nothing and the man who comes to him to ask him to insure knows everything, it is the duty of the assured, the man who desires to have a policy, to make a disclosure to the underwriters without being asked of all the material circumstances, because the underwriters know nothing and the assured knows everything."* Scrutton L J. Rozanes v Bowen [1928]

"The Courts require the strictest good faith in policies of assurance" Mackenzie v Coulson *[1869]*.

The duty of utmost good faith is required from both the assured and the insurer. There are old established cases in support but the recent case, *La Banque Financiere v Westgate Insurance* [1986] appealed *Banque Keyser Ullman v Skandia Insurance* [1988] and finally before the House of Lords, I suggest is not helpful as the contrary decisions at the levels of the Courts, at which the decisions emanated provide some confusion. Further, it seems that the probable fact that the insurance was a "guarantee" and thus the principle of utmost good faith not applicable in full was not canvassed.

There are some matters that need not be disclosed. i.e.

[1] The existence of other insurances. *McDonnell v Beacon Fire* [1857]
[2] Facts the disclosure of which would have only caused delay *Mutual Life of New York v Ontario Metal Products* [1925]
[3] Previous breaches of duty. *C.T.I. v Oceanus* [1984]
[4] Over insurance (but not deliberate and intentional) even if not shown to be fraudulent.

The support arises from Marine cases and as normal material damage and interruption insurances are subject to "average" it may well be that it would be necessary to establish fraud, itself a reason to void a policy, for this rule to be applied to these two classes of insurance.

[5] Facts which diminish the risk. *Carter v Boehm* [1894]

This is perhaps regarding the cover as one. Thus an empty, or silent, premises may have less "occupation" hazards but an increased exposure to vandals etc. and it would be a matter of opinion what the overall effect is. However, if the cover is by way of a "combined" policy with the sections separately rated it may be that each section would be affected on their own merit. See page 37.

[6] circumstances known, or reasonably presumed known, to the insurer. The insurer is presumed to know matters of common notoriety or knowledge, those which an insurer ought to know from his activities as such. *Carter v Boehm* [1894]

[7] That which is not required by reason of an express or implied warranty or has been waived.

[8] That which the insurer should reasonably infer from that disclosed to him. *Bates v Hewitt* [1867]

C. APPLICATION OF THE PRINCIPLE

The rule of disclosure applies from the inception of the cover and then at each renewal of it. Alterations during currency are a matter of a policy condition, see Section 5.

This introduces two factors:

(i) The relationship between the parties
(ii) The class of insurance concerned.

These are now discussed.

Party relationships

These are between [i] The Insured and his advisers and [ii] The Insurer and their Agents if so acting. The duty applies to both sides although, in practical terms, most of the matters involved call for the Insured to provide the necessary information. That which is "material" will depend on the class of insurance, that which an insurer should, of his own volition, know and that which is needed to be advised; that which the insurer specifically requests, often by a proposal form - but it may be orally by his officials at various stages up to the conclusion of the contract, that which the insurer by his actions or advices waives, e.g. limited period of advice re claims experience on the proposal form whether used or not. Thus insurers in larger cases, or with industrial processes etc involved, commonly obtain a survey report, usually by their own trained staff and this, added to the normal expectance that the insurer is aware of the hazards of trades, construction, services, machinery etc. allows the Insured to limit his advices to either the very unusual, if that is not apparent and to correctly answer points raised.

For interruption insurance cases disclosure includes the physical hazards, although these may be known if the material damage insurance is placed with the same insurers that carry the interruption risk. In general, the aspects of geographical, economic, social and taxation etc. are matters that a competent insurer should know, or he is on general warning to ask.

Some additional perils may call for additional disclosure, but the common features of weather conditions etc. are matters which are for the insurers to ascertain.

Difficulties can arise regarding past ownership of a company, its financial results and trading history etc. but in general, if facts are given it is for the insurer to pursue the data if greater knowledge is wanted.

For the larger Company, especially the multi-national major, the details of what is relevant is not easy to determine as changes often occur in the constituents of the organisation and the past history of losses may not be fully known, particularly if the new overall organisation insures for a wider range of perils than the acquired organisation. Whilst the duty of disclosure is only that which is known, this is not limited to exclude that which should in the normal course of business be in the knowledge of a company. It also raises the question at what level of management this knowledge should be held and below which it is not knowledge of the insured. This relationship needs to be clearly agreed by the parties beforehand to avoid subsequent problems.

There are now agents, who not being registered as Insurance Brokers with the recognised bodies, may be treated as representatives of the insurer. In these cases information known to them, whether from the insured or by other means, will be knowledge known to the insurer, whether disclosed to them or not. In like manner an Agent of the Insured is required to advise the insurer that which is relevant and in his knowledge whether the facts are given to him by the Insured or from their own knowledge.

Where multi-purpose insurance brokers are involved the matter may be complicated if different sections of that organisation are involved. It may be alleged that information to one such sector is not available to another because of the responsibility to each sections clients is individual. Hence the phrase "Chinese walls" that are required to be maintained.

The class of insurance concerned

It is necessary not only to consider the class of insurance involved and to determine what are material facts relating to them but whether it is a direct insurance or a matter of reinsurance and then if by a treaty arrangement, which will be governed largely by its terms or a one-off facultative case, where greater detail is normally required. However, in these cases the fact that both parties are professionals in the matter can give greater responsibility on each to appreciate the meaning of abbreviated data and the conclusions that can be understood from these such as the level of rate to indicate the exposure. A higher rate than normal, especially for acceptances of off-shore insurances of itself indicates some adverse feature(s) and the acceptor is, to some extent, put on warning and failure to enquire may indicate waiver of disclosure of additional matter.

It is also relevant that acceptances of overseas insurances will represent acceptance of the legal rulings of the country where primarily underwriting has taken place. The acceptor will be required to follow on that basis and not rely on English law if it differs The case *Forsikorings Vesta v Butcher* [1986] deals with the aspects involved.

Combined or packet policies

These are normally a single contract but the conditions divided between those relating to a section of the cover, material damage, interruption, liability etc. and those headed "General" which apply to the whole. Breach of a condition normally affects the whole contract irrespective of the extent of its application to the actual claim. Here, however, it seems likely, dependant on the wording actually used, that breach will affect either the section or the whole based on that which is breached. A recent law case *Printpak v A.G.F. Insurance Ltd* [1999] confirms this.

Long term agreements

The acceptance by the parties of a long term agreement to renew the insurance for a period of years would normally extend the time during which the duty of disclosure is non applicable, as such.

D. INTERRUPTION INSURANCE ASPECTS

It must be remembered that as a separate class of insurance the requirements of disclosure may, in practical terms, differ when an interruption insurance is involved. For example:

- [a] The insured, more often than not, will be a Plc or Limited Company and the knowledge that it must disclose is that known to itself - that will include management, and
- [b] The trading position in the past might be held to be material in a special case, but for larger trading organisations a matter of general knowledge.

It is however, difficult to envisage the trading position being relevant to the underwriting of a cover on the modern standard form which provides for businesses trading at a net loss.

General market conditions, overall or relative to certain industries or sections of the economy, and the published results or trading companies and the like, and the public knowledge set out in financial papers are all factors of knowledge of which a competent Underwriter should be aware.

See further comments at Section 5.

E. DISCLOSURE OF A CRIMINAL RECORD

A recent case *Constantinou v Aegon Insce. Co. and Stevenson Price* [1995] gives a current Court view on this matter. The non admission of liability by the insurer was on two counts [a] ...... and [b] non disclosure of past convictions outside the Rehabilitation of Offenders Act 1974 legislation spent cases limits.

Two past law cases were cited:

[i] *Schoolman v Hall* [1951]
"Jeweller had as a young man been convicted of larceny on six occasions over a period of seven years ending fourteen years before the date of the policy. A jury found that these were material facts and

the Court of Appeal refused to disturb this finding, despite the fact that the assured's record related to a "dim and remote past" [comment by Asquith, L.J.]

[ii] *Reynolds v Phoenix Assurance Co* [1978]

"In interlocutory proceedings Lord Denning, M.R. had thought it debatable whether a conviction of 10 years standing for receiving resulting in a fine ought to be disclosed and Forbes, J. held at the trial that it was not material.

These decisions were before the House of Lords rulings in *Pan Atlantic v Pine Top* [1994]

In "Constantinou" the past convictions (while serious in themselves - armed robbery; fraudulent conversion; forgery and/or obtaining money by false pretences) were in excess of 20 years prior to the effecting of the policy the subject of the claim for "Fire".

The Judge at first instance declined to rule that [b] was applicable.

The case has been appealed to the House of Lords via the Court of Appeal but this was restricted to point [a] .... The Insurers appealed under [b] but on appeal this was rejected as out of time (originally allowed by a Master).

No published record of this case is at present known.

SECTION 5

ALTERATION OF RISK DURING THE POLICY CURRENCY

"Times change and we change with them." - Harrison [1597]

Once a contract has been completed then it will continue for its agreed duration, see Section 4.

However, this position will be affected if:

(a) The basis of the contract is changed

or

(b) There are provisions in it regarding matters that must be agreed if they arise.

It is perhaps unfortunate that there is not a current major textbook which sets out in detail the legal aspects of "Disclosure", "Non disclosure" and "Alteration of Risk" during the currency of the policy. The standard work, now out of print, Welford and Otter - Barry was last reprinted in 1948 and gives some 22 pages to this subject with numerous law cases cited.

Under sub heading (a) above, the position re material damage insurances can be ascertained from two cases.

[i] *Baxendale v Harvey* [1859] per Pollock C.B
[ii] *Thompson v Hopper* [1858] per Willes J.

stating: "In effect, there being no violation of the law and no fraud on behalf of the Assured, an increase of risk to the subject matter of insurance, its identity remaining, though such increased risk be caused by the assured, if it be not prohibited by the policy, does not avoid the insurance."

Thus it is with reference to the description of the subject matter contained in the policy that direct attention needs to be given.

With regard to sub heading [b] above, the "Alteration of Risk" provisions are set out as a condition in the standard material damage insurance policy, being part of a general condition worded as follows:

2. ALTERATION

"This policy shall be avoided with respect to any of the property insured in regard to which there may be any alteration after the commencement of the insurance

(a) *by removal or*
(b) *whereby the risk of DAMAGE is increased or*
(c) *whereby the interest of the Insured ceases except by will or operation of law unless admitted by the Insurer in writing."*

Thus under the material damage insurance the effect of this condition will have a bearing on the aspect of the application of the material damage provision as will apply under the counterpart interruption insurance.

It is then separately necessary to consider the position under the interruption policy. Here the policy condition reads:

"This policy shall be void if after the commencement of this insurance

- [a] *the Business be wound up or carried on by a liquidator or receiver or permanently discontinued or*
- [b] *any alteration be made either in the Business or in the Premises or Property therein whereby the risk of loss, destruction or damage is increased, unless admitted by the Insurer in writing."*

Thus we have two factors:

- [i] alteration to the Businesses and
- [ii] alteration to the Premises/Property therein
whereby the "risk" is increased.

Under the material damage condition the word "risk" refers to the chance of the event happening and not to the property itself. Under the interruption policy condition the wording implies that it is not the risk of the event but the alteration which increases the risk that has to be advised. Whether this in practice will affect any individual case is unclear and it may be that so far as this sub-section is concerned it is referring to the material damage rate that applies to the Premises or Property. It will be observed that no reference is made at that point to the aspect of a change in the "interruption" factors to which a business is exposed.

However, there is the first sub-section that specifically refers to an alteration in the Business whereby the risk of loss is increased. This would seem to limit this not, to the general interruption factors, but more limited to a change in the nature of the Business as insured.

SECTION 6

A CHANGE IN PARTICIPATION OF INSURERS DURING THE CURRENCY OF THE POLICY

"The rarity of law cases in respect of interruption insurance may perhaps give rise to the lawyer world, the belief that opportunities for business are passing them by"

Recently a legal luminary in a case put forward his view that such an event meant that a new contract had arisen and that the duty of disclosure of material facts to the insurers, both new and old, arose.

The facts of the case were:

- [a] A material damage policy underwritten by two insurers in equal proportions.
- [b] The property was a building and there was a requirement for full insurance.
- [c] The property was revalued during currency and a large increase in sum insured was requested to meet this valuation.
- [d] The two insurers desired to reduce their participation by 50% and five new insurers were added each being advised the name of the leading insurer.
- [e] The insurance was continued by the now seven insurers with the existing long-term agreement, in standard form and terms etc. as before.

A legal case was quoted, *Methol v Argonaut Marine Insce. Co. Ltd* [1925] but this related to marine insurance. It will be appreciated that under a material damage policy the indemnity is determined at the date of the insured event and the sum insured is merely a maximum limit. Under a marine insurance on a hull the sum insured at the inception is related to the indemnity payable as well as other considerations applying.

There is, in my view no reason to regard the marine decision as a precedent or applying to material damage or interruption insurances. Thus, there is no new insurance effected by the two existing insurers who continue at a lower participation, although at their decision the amount of their participation was somewhat higher than before in monetary terms and the increase was as required by the policy terms to be for the current value. The new insurers were at their own onus to investigate any details, re disclosure, from the existing lead insurer, which in fact they had done and make their decision on participation on that information. It would appear therefore that there was no responsibility of disclosure by the insured to the new insurers within the overall period of the long-term agreement.

SECTION 7

CONTRIBUTION DOUBLE "RENT" COVERS

"Rent, being a Business Charge, is therefore most properly covered by inclusion as an item of Fixed Charges"
Younger G.W - Extract from the "Secretary" 1920.

Apportionment of Rent between Fire and Consequential Loss policies - Huddart R.M.F. 1926 in booklet "Consequential Loss."

"It was evidently not originally intended that Consequential Loss Policies should relieve fire policies of any part of the latter's liability for rent, nor can it be ignored that these two policies insure essentially different aspects of the rent loss; on the other hand precedent is all powerful in insurance matters and it has been suggested that as rent figures in both policies in some form or other, the rent loss should accordingly, be apportioned. It is difficult, however, to find any common basis of apportionment between them as whilst the indemnity under the Consequential Loss policy depends upon the drop in the earnings, the rent insurance under the fire policy depends on the untenantability of the premises. Further the two policies are not concurrent in respect of time."

(a) The subject matter of insurance must be common to all the policies. They need not be for the same amount or that the scope of cover is the same.
(b) The policies must include the common peril involved
(c) The policies must cover a common interest - the community of interest arises. Where separate insurances have been effected by different parties then the question of the intention of the insurance protection for whom arises - if common interest then contribution may arise, if different, then no contribution is involved.

There are a number of law cases in respect of "non rent" insurances which have dealt with this issue to which detailed reference is advisable if a specific case arising under which these aspects need clarification.

In respect of alleged double "Rent" insurance several points initially arise.

(a) Is the cover to protect a common interest or not? A "fire" material damage type policy on rent may or may not indicate the nature of the "rent" protected. i.e. rent payable or rent receivable, or even rent of an alternative property whilst the insured premises are untenantable. The further "rent" insurance may be for a separate party. Both covers may be for different time periods and amounts but neither of these points are material to the question of contribution.

(b) Is the policy provision for indemnity common in form? It is usual for a material damage type cover to be governed by the following provisions:

    [i] the amount insured to be an indemnity pro rata to the stated period of rent cover in the policy.

[ii] this pro rata sum to be payable for the time period that the insured premises was untenantable, or such other phrase used, but not exceeding the stated period insured.

[iii] the general principle of indemnity.

Under an interruption cover on the standard type wording the loss is measured by a set down formula with precision. Provided the term "Gross Profit" (or equivalent) includes within its' scope "Rent" then the loss calculation within its whole may provide some indemnity by way of rent. It may not as:

(a) A reduction in turnover is needed to trigger the formula and the claim maybe one of "increased costs of working" only.
(b) Savings in rent will be deducted and these could reduce the actual indemnity re rent, to nil.
(c) The policy may provide for damage at premises other than those of the insured to allow for indemnity to arise, the rent policy would not normally operate in such a case.

The position of a tenant or lessee may be involved and the principle established in *Rowlands Ltd v Berni Inns* [1985] may need to be considered.

Conclusion

(a) Where the two policies are of the same type and class the normal rules re "contribution" will apply.
(b) Where the two covers are of a different class of insurance, property/interruption, there will not be contribution between them as such.

However

[i] the material damage policy will be subject to the general principle of indemnity.
[ii] the payment under the material damage policy may have to be brought into consideration as a saving under the interruption policy terms. (Policy Condition 3 – Contribution.)

SUPPLEMENT

"M2K" OR MILLENNIUM "BUG" PROBLEMS

Experto credite - Aneid -Virgil

The DATE RECOGNITION CLAUSE

This matter is discussed by means of a supplement as that which is available consists of (1) the clause set out below which may differ between insurers and be varied in the light of any circumstances arising, and (2) because there are no legal decisions on its correct interpretation.

Date Recognition Clause

There is no insurance under this policy in respect of any claim of whatsoever nature which arises directly or indirectly from or consists of the failure or inability of any

(a) Electronic circuit, microchip, integrated circuit, microprocessor, embedded system, hardware, software, firmware, program, computer data processing equipment, telecommunication equipment or systems and similar devices

(b) Media or systems used in connection with any of the foregoing whether the property of the insured or not, at any time to achieve any or all of the purposes and consequential effects intended by the use of any number, symbol or word to denote a date, including, without limitation, the failure or inability to recognise, capture, save retain or restore and/or correctly manipulate, interpret, transmit, return, calculate, or process any date, data, information, command, logic or instruction as a result of:

(i) recognising, using or adopting any date, day of the week or period of time otherwise than as, or other than, the true or correct date, day of the week or period of time

(ii) the operation of any command or logic which has been programmed or incorporated into anything referred to in (a) and (b) above.

Provided always that this clause shall not apply to claims otherwise indemnifiable under this policy, subject to all its terms and provisions comprising loss or destruction of, or damage to, property owned by, in the possession of or held in trust by the insured and/or the insured's consequential losses arising from loss or destruction of or damage to any property if directly caused by fire, lightning, explosion, aircraft and other aerial devices or articles dropped therefrom, riot, civil commotion, strikers, locked out workers, persons taking part in labour disturbances, malicious persons other than thieves, earthquake, storm, flood, escape of water from any tank apparatus or pipe, impact by any road vehicle or animal or theft

For the avoidance of doubt the foregoing exemption to this clause shall not apply to any claim arising from any legal liability of the insured

This clause does not apply to any claim arising under insurance in respect of "Employers' Liability" or "Personal Accident" if provided by this Policy.

It is important for intermediaries to appreciate that they may have a liability arising from lack of advice to their clients on this subject but for those clients and their staff to realise that such failure may not create any indemnity from an intermediary if, in fact, the failure, while confirmed, does not give rise to any recovery as no insurance to provide such protection could have been obtained. It might be however, that some liability could be established, as even without an insurance market for such a cover, the Insured could have established internally some financial funding to provide for the financial loss arising, or dealt with it through mutual or offshore insurance arrangements.

While reputable U.K. insurers have a long history of treating policy provisions with due regard to common sense although drafting conditions on an excessive exclusion basis, it is not acceptable under modern circumstances to rely on this continuing in the future or that their example will be adopted by all the market insurers that may be involved.

An example of the divergence of thought that exists is shown in a pamphlet by one major U K insurer in which it is stated:

"In some instances - for example, material damage policies - insurers will provide cover for certain consequences of a failure of a chip to recognise the date change."

"In other instances - most notably breakdown and certain liability covers - there will be no cover available to clients at all."

Whereas elsewhere in that pamphlet it is stated

"Quite simply, most events arising from Y2K are inevitable. And therefore, by careful planning and thinking ahead could be avoided."

"Overall, the insurance industry takes the view that it is not in business to cover losses which are clearly avoidable. Which means that it is very much in the interests of your clients to take as many steps as possible to prevent identifiable problems arising."

"It is particularly important that you and your staff understand this clause. You should note that a central feature of this definition is that it only relates to failure of chips and computer programs to recognise a date change and that this not only includes year 2000 but also any other dates that may cause problems."

"For these and other property classes, customers will still have the protection against loss or damage by fire and defined perils where these have occurred as a result of a Y2K failure."

"How does this apply in practice? If, for example, a central heating system fails to work, or is damaged because it is not 2000 compliant, then the system is not covered.

However, if as a result there is water damage to the property, this will be covered, provided of course, that water damage is an insured peril and that the customer has complied with the policy terms and conditions."

"As far as intruder detector, fire alarm, sprinkler systems and the like are concerned the onus is on your customers to ensure that they are Year 2000 compliant. If they do not do so, their cover may well be invalidated, because of the standard warranty or the 'reasonable precautions' clause.

A close reading of these notes show gaps exist and too broad statements are given when individual aspects are considered as will be seen from the following comments. These deal only with the matter relative to Property and Interruption insurances in the U.K. and this work is limited to considerations in respect of such insurances only.

1. THE GENERAL LEGAL POSITION RELATING TO MATERIAL DAMAGE POLICIES

(a) The policy is one of indemnity in respect of a fortuitous event by a peril insured. Thus, as this term fortuitous may not include that which is 'accidental' (which involves engineering type covers), there the term 'Sudden and unforeseen damage' is normal.

The cover does not exclude 'negligence' events as such, nor is there a requirement for the Insured to take reasonable precautions.

Wilful actions

There are several cases (see the notes at the end hereof) that show that the English Courts will not allow the inclusion of a 'reasonable precautions clause' for insurers to avoid liability unless, as a matter of fact, which is at the Courts discretion, the lack of precaution is 'wilful'. A policy condition may also apply as set out later. Thus to imply more than this is incorrect, and it seems to me likely that the English Courts will follow a similar attitude re the Date Recognition Clause.

2. INSURED PERILS AND PROXIMATE CAUSE

The normal U.K. property and Interruption policies do NOT incorporate the word "directly" relative to the cover being afforded. For property insurances the matter is dealt with by legal precedent cases and for interruption policies it would be self-defeating the consequential nature of the cover provided. Thus in the opening paragraph of the Date Recognition Clause the use of the phrase "directly or indirectly" introduces a conflict.

So far as an interruption policy is concerned the use of this phrase in the "Nuclear Explosion" provisions gave rise to necessity for it to be redrafted by a preliminary phrase to that used in property and other covers. This will be discussed further later.

3. The Insurer's Statement

The statement "Insurers are not in business to cover losses which are clearly avoidable" is trite. All losses to a business can be avoided if it closes down. Industry, commerce and business is conducted and its activities involve risks. Shareholders are aware of this and expect management to protect them in respect of those unexpected events for which traditionally the U.K. Insurers have provided insurance and to seek the widest cover compatible to their needs in a modern and enlightened market place. The extent of the cover frequently is for "All Risks" and here the exceptions to the cover are set down. These exceptions have to be considered in the light of the basic legal aspect of insurance in that it excludes that which is not fortuitous or accidental (the line between these may not always be clear). It is reasonable for this line to be set down but it should not exclude available cover for some aspects even if this involves the traditional "Fire" property policy and an additional "Breakdown" insurance.

The avoidance of Y2K events are not always "inevitable" as is acknowledged and neither can the actual insured always be able to avoid the exposure when the electronic equipment etc. is controlled by others. It is not necessarily always a matter that recovery can be made against other parties, nor the expense in respect of major organisations such as public authorities alleged negligence a light matter to undertake.

1. REVIEW BY EXAMPLES

Perhaps the best way of illustrating the aspects of the cover under insurance material damage and interruption policies and that which will be excluded by the new policy Date Recognition Clause is to focus on examples relative to the areas of the case likely to be affected. It is stressed that considerations of liabilities that may arise in these cases upon third parties are not reviewed.

Example A

A private householder

(a) domestic equipment possibly involved, such as refrigerators, washing machines and the like. The effect seems likely to be limited to excluding damage to the equipment itself and subsequent damage to the contents.

The effect would seem to be the rendering valueless of cover on the items of equipment and/or loss to the contents by the Y2K failure of the equipment. Thus the limitation to the cover is applicable to those insurances which provide some protection to loss of the contents of refrigerators from their malfunction or failure and this seems intentional but the financial amounts likely to be involved are small and the failure probably ascertainable in time for salvage action to be applied by the householder.

(b) Items of electronic equipment used by the family, such as, fax, computer/word processors and the like.

Again the damage or uselessness of the item of equipment itself will be excluded but it is unlikely that any cover existed in any case. The spread of damage from such an event as in the above examples, would remain to the extent that such damage is insured. The exception to this statement would turn on if a narrow view of the words of the clause were to be put forward, i.e. The proviso that the clause does not apply if the loss occurs by a named and insured peril otherwise in the cover and directly arising therefrom is compared with the opening exclusion of loss directly or indirectly from the failure. Thus if the failure does cause a heating up of the item of equipment and subsequently this involves a fire, there will be surrounding damage from the heat, which is not a named peril, and then fire damage - which to property already damaged by heat - could be said not to have given rise to any further monetary loss and then other property from which a claim could be admissible in full. That is unless the "indirectly" exclusion is considered to have some part to play and provide an exclusion to operate. It is considered that such a widespread interpretation of the application of the word "indirectly" should not be applied. Generally "Damage" by fire is covered by insurance irrespective of its originating cause except those which are specifically excluded, i.e. war risks etc. Where the policy is extended to provide some form of "All Risks" cover the adding back of the named peril protection may not adequately express the cover that should continue.

Example B

The Professional person, Solicitor, Architect, Surveyor, Engineer, Dentist, Doctor and the like

The equipment used by these is widespread and thus more items could be affected by this kind of event. The damage to the equipment will be excluded and as in Example A the surrounding loss aspect arises with similar comments applicable but augmented in that associated equipment may frequently be involved and if situated close by that in which the failure occurs, the differentiation of heat and then fire damage will be an important factor. Damage arising to computers and the like; records may be involved with similar considerations of the extent of the cover applying if no fire or other named event happens. Generally this loss would appear to be intentionally excluded, even where a wider cover than from named perils has been given under the existing insurance. The problem of what reconstruction of data is needed, the cost involved as actual and research etc. and the value of the records as such will need to be faced and to the extent there is cover provisions relating to these matters that will apply.

Where wider than named perils cover is in existence the adding back proviso of the clause, coupled with the "indirect" opening paragraph exclusion may allow a very wide opportunity for some insurers to maintain a strong line of limiting the cover that existed previously. The clause being additional and added later to the contract would in normal circumstances be held to dominate.

Example C
Small shops and the like

In these, small electronic equipment is increasingly to be found and as time passes its involvement in stock control is added to the original control of recording sales etc.

In addition to the points indicated in Examples A and B will be the extent, if, following fire damage, the loss of the records will interfere with the interruption insurance claim especially where on the proposal form reference is made to the maintenance of accounting records etc. The use in the opening paragraph of "indirectly" introduces the ability for an insurer to reduce or exclude a loss on this basis.

Additionally, the heating or malfunctioning of the electronic equipment can give rise to the condemnation of susceptible stock either as a general precaution or by the decision of a local authority. Such loss would seem to be excluded, even if for example fire ensued or not.

Example D
Larger organisations but not multi-national or international companies.

The exposures to be considered comprise three main areas:

(1)   The property aspect of the insurer's premises.

   Here the risk may relate to equipment of the insured which will follow the remarks previously set out, or those of a landlord etc. in respect of which the Insured has no direct knowledge. The failure of heating equipment involves not only the boilers etc. and the specialist equipment likely to involve the Y2K hazards, which will be a matter for the party responsible for it, but the possible cessation of the operation of the activities of the business through the premises not being kept at the required condition either for personnel or the trade process. If this arises, solely from the failure without a specific peril ensuing, there is no cover, but if from the failure there is subsequent damage by such a peril what is the actual cover?

   The subsequent paragraph adds back some protection but does this override the loss that is inevitable from the failure of the equipment itself and by the word "indirect" does this then further operate as an exclusion? The rule re loss flowing from two events virtually simultaneously is the subject of comments elsewhere in this work but as there set down turns mainly upon whether one event is a "non insured" matter when the insured cover will predominate or an "excluded" peril event which then will override the named peril cover.

   The position may also give rise to consideration of "Rent etc." liabilities between the parties which will be a detailed matter of the terms of the actual agreement in force. The leases often involve requirements of insurance but it may be the position of a non mentioned or non insured event that has to be considered, and determining on whom the loss will fall.

(2) The risks arising from the insurer's own, or hired in, equipment which will be, as indicated previously, except that for leased or hired in equipment responsibilities may also involve considerations of the hiring contract.

(3) The dependence of the business on others, a matter relating to the interruption policy of the Insured.

This for general supplies usually does not involve contracts but there can be exceptions which would then require consideration of the supply contract. The cause of the non supply will probably be a matter of concern to the extent there is cover and the onus of proof falling on whom when this is not clear? *Prima facie,* normally under an interruption policy the onus of proof will fall on the insurer once a reduction in turnover/or increase in cost of working has ensued. (see elsewhere in this work re this).

There are often extensions to public supply authorities and these not only involve equal aspects as just outlined, but include the fact that the cover wording may refer to failure of current at the terminal ends of the supply system, subject to an excess or franchise period. It seems unreasonable that such a specific form of cover should be brought into doubt by an overall policy exclusion clause involving factors beyond the control of the insured. Thus where Engineering policies are involved, both material damage cover as well as those involving interruption protection, a specific review of the effect and intention of the insurer is essential.

Example E
Multi-national or International Organisations

These companies will be aware of the problems inherent in their electronic etc. systems and have professional insurance advisers. Thus, bearing in mind that usually purpose designed covers apply with large deductibles, the extent to which the Date Recognition clause is applicable can be reviewed specifically in each case and provided the general points previously made are considered, the necessary action can be taken to resolve the loss possibilities to be faced. Possibly it is the interruption factors that are the predominant features to be closely reviewed and the financial maximum exposure that could arise, bearing in mind that "customer" reaction could be involved.

2. AN ALTERNATIVE POLICY CLAUSE

The basic feature arising is not a new one. Machinery and plant etc. have always been subject to "internal" events outside the scope of a policy drafted to provide protection from named perils. An "electrical" clause is normally a part of the Specification to property insurance for industrial Insured. Strangely this clause is not part of the "Recommended" standard U.K. policy, nor is its wording exactly common, although with scheduled insurances with participating insurers, that normally used by the leader is followed without comment.

This clause is not intended to do more than make clear the exclusion from the cover of damage by the internal breakdown of equipment in respect of the item of equipment in question involved and subsequent damage is not excluded by the clause. This may explain the anomaly that the clause is not universally found in property insurances such as office etc. cases. As discussed elsewhere in this work, the clause is also not often found in a standard U.K. interruption insurance policy and problems do arise where both "internal" excluded damage and subsequent "insured peril" damage arises. Usually fire or explosion.

It might be thought that a common approach to these two aspects with universal application to all named peril property and interruption insurances would be appropriate in modern conditions when electronic etc. equipment is to be found in the home, offices, small businesses as well as the larger organisations.

The following draft wording indicates a clarification on these lines:

Electronic equipment and the like plant etc. Definition of cover clause

This policy does not cover loss resulting from DAMAGE to Property occasioned by:

    [i]   its own spontaneous fermentation or heating or its undergoing any process involving the application of heat

    [ii] any dynamo, motor, transformer, machine or other apparatus caused by its own over-running, excessive pressure, short circuiting, self-heating or leakage of electricity.

    [iii] any failure or inability of any

(a) electronic circuit, microchip, integrated circuit, microprocessor, embedded system, hardware, software, firmware, program, computer data processing equipment, telecommunication equipment, or systems and similar devises

(b) media or systems used in connection with any item listed under (a) above.

whether the property of the Insured or not, at any time in consequence of its failure or inability to achieve any, or all of, the purposes and consequential effects intended by the use of any number, symbol or word to denote a date, including without limitation, the failure or inability to recognise, capture, save, retain, restore and/or correctly manipulate, interpret, transmit, return, calculate or process any date, data, information, command, logic or instruction as a result of:

(1) recognising, using or adopting any date, day of the week or period of time otherwise than as, or other than, the true or correct date, day of the week or period of time.

(2) the operation of any command or logic which has been programmed or incorporated into anything referred to in (a) and (b) above, but this shall not exclude (i) such DAMAGE not otherwise excluded which itself results

from an Insured or Defined Peril or (ii) subsequent Damage which results from a cause not otherwise excluded.

Specific comment on this Draft clause.

(i) it follows existing policy provisions format and avoids possible debate on whether variations in the format used in this area involve differences in cover provided.

(ii) the Claims Condition of the "recommended" standard property and interruption policies provides for exclusion of loss caused by "the wilful act or connivance of the Insured" and this would seem adequate and more correct in the setting out of this exclusion than requirement to take reasonable precautions and more in line with the legal rulings that apply thereto

(iii) there are a number of exclusions set down in an "All Risks" "recommended" U.K. policy form such as "disappearance" and erasures....the new provision must not override these. The adding back provision in the proposed Date Recognition clause of loss from specific perils leaves two problems:

(a) What of insured events wider than those set down
(b) Proximate loss events which are within the current policy cover but may be considered excluded by the extreme width of the proposed clause.

(iv) Interruption insurance policies (by whatever name is used)

The problem inherent in the use of widely defined exclusion clauses was established when the Nuclear Fission Exclusion provision was first introduced and initially indicated to apply with a common wording. This is detailed in the booklet "Interruption Insurance - Proximate Loss Issues " by G.J.R. Hickmott, first published in 1990 and subsequently reprinted. Without some modification an existing fully insured loss could be affected materially by such terms. The market resolved the problem by the use of an introductory phrase which is echoed by its continued inclusion where combined wordings are used as follows:

"For the purpose of this section (Section 2 - Business Interruption) the words "This policy does not cover" in Condition [2] [b] of the policy shall read "This policy does not cover loss resulting from damage occasioned by or happening through or occasioning".i.e. it is the prime damage event that has to be involved not the position arising after an insured event has been established. The alternative wording set out above achieves this, it is thought, by referring at the outset to "Damage".

To amplify this by an example:

An insured event occurs and the policy is triggered to provide indemnity by its terms. During the insured indemnity period a Y2K event occurs outside negligence of the Insured either at the "Premises" or under an appropriate extension cover or elsewhere to prejudice the earlier recovery of the business and this aggravates the existing insured loss. By the proposed wording this aggravation would appear to have to be excluded in the financial settlement. If the market continues to provide protection in the event of a Nuclear Fission event to the extent shown, it seems harsh without specific warning to apply stricter terms for Y2K events.

Final review of the position at this stage when little reaction from others is known

1. The draft proposed wording may or may not be followed by all insurers as wordings are free now with the non existence of a "Tariff" association. This is however a weakness as the previous market discussions would have taken place and the view of Insureds would have been sought and registered.

2. If other than one agreed wording in fact emerges then confusion is likely and it will be more difficult to comment on comparative policy situations.

3. There are events, beyond the appreciation of an Insured, and for which it is not unreasonable for him to seek insurance protection, which appears to have been excluded from an existing normal policy cover. Should these and also those to which attention has now been drawn, not be matters for which the market will provide protection either by extension to existing insurance policies or by a separate cover, at an appropriate premium?

4. The Office of Fair Trading has a responsibility to ensure that the outcome in this matter is correct, both for an International and United Kingdom approach, bearing their insistence of the freedom to be at all times existent in the market place; yet the fairness of the protection of people and industry needs to be insured.

5. As given by an individual, the comments are limited as such and the examples cannot be fully comprehensive nor the intentions of insurers determined. The comments are only, at this stage, the misgivings that arise as indicated and the problem of universal agreement on the intention and application need to be faced. If the U.K. is to maintain its stated role as world leader in at least the technical fields of insurance, it is considered more is needed to be done.

   Thus, I can only set down these views, without prejudice, and with readers being asked to apply their problems to the aspects that they either foresee or need to investigate.

Notes:

Legal cases re "reasonable precautions" clauses

There are numerous cases applicable arising from various types of property insurance and other classes and the following are some of them:

Aluminium Wire & Cable v Allstate Ins. Co. Ltd. [1958]
Fraser v B.N. Furman (Productions) Ltd. [1967]
Beauchamp v National Mutual Indemnity Ins. Co. [1937]

Woodfall and Rimmer v Moyle [1942]   Exclusion of Wilful acts.
City Tailors v Evans [1921]
Beresford v Royal Ins. Co. [1938]

The comments of Diplock, L.J. perhaps is indicative of the overall outlook.

"What, in my judgement, is reasonable as between the insured and the insurer, without being repugnant to the commercial purpose of the contract is that the insured where he does recognise a danger should not deliberately court it by taking measures that he himself knows are inadequate to avert it. In other words, it is not enough that the employer's omission to take any particular precautions to avoid accidents should be negligent; it must at least be reckless, that is to say, made with the actual recognition by the Insured himself that a danger exists, and not caring whether or not it is averted. The purpose of the condition is to ensure that the Insured will not, because he is covered against the loss by the policy, refrain from taking precautions which he knows ought to be taken.

APPENDIX I

THE STANDARD INTERRUPTION INSURANCE POLICY IN THE U.K.

1. The current position in the U.K. is that there is no market agreement to a compulsory policy wording for normal interruption insurances, but the Association of British Insurers (ABI) have adopted a "recommended" wording which is in common usage by most of its members, although there may be minor alterations to suit the layout they prefer etc.

2. The A.B.I. also has set out a number of wordings as recommended for use to provide additional cover, such as perils, extensions, clauses etc. These are in common use by many insurers.

3. Insurers with Overseas head offices, other non-member insurers etc. may or may not adopt the "recommended" wordings in whole or part.

4. This creates a problem for any Adviser or the Insured himself, in being able to easily establish the extent to which the cover is standard or what variation therefrom applies. The Office of Fair Trading and others who might well realise the need to provide some regular basis seem to have no interest in this matter. In overseas countries registration of policy wordings may be required.

A simple control could be introduced which would reduce many aspects of this matter. i.e. the agreed basic standard wording to be recognised as such and to this extent the policy wording would be printed in BLACK. Any extra cover can be added by an insurer but the additional protection would be by printed matter in GREEN. Any reduction in the cover would need to be printed in RED. Any policy print in BLACK would be deemed to provide cover as stated but never less than the standard policy provisions.

Thus the Insured or any Broker, or other adviser could rely on the fact that the cover as shown is that of a standard form unless and to the extent that RED or GREEN printed matter is set down.

STANDARD FIRE BUSINESS INTERRUPTION POLICY.

The Insurer agrees (subject to the terms, definition, exclusions and conditions of this policy) that if after payment of the first premium any building or other property used by the insured at the Premises for the purpose of the Business be lost destroyed or damaged by

1. FIRE but excluding loss destuction or damage caused by
   - (a) Explosion resulting from fire
   - (b) Earthquake or subterranean fire,
   - (c) (i) its own spontaneous fermentation or heating, or
     - (ii) its undergoing any heating process or any process involving the application of heat

2. LIGHTNING
3. EXPLOSION
    (a) Of boilers used for domestic purposes only
    (b) Of any other boilers or economisers on the Premises
    (c) Of gas used for domestic purposes only

    but excluding loss destruction or damage caused by earthquake or subterranean fire

    during the period of insurance (or any subsequent period for which the Insurer accepts a renewal premium) and in consequence the Business carried on by the Insured at the Premises be interrupted or interfered with then the Insurer will pay to the Insured in respect of each item in the schedule the amount of loss resulting from such interruption or interference provided that

    1. at the time of the happening of the loss destruction or damage there shall be in force an insurance covering the interest of the insured in the property at the premises against such loss destruction or damage and that
        (i) payment shall have been made or liability admitted therefor, or
        (ii) payment would have been made or liability admitted therefor but for the operation of a proviso in such insurance excluding liability for losses below a specified amount
    2. the liability of the insurer under this policy shall not exceed
        (i) in the whole the total sum insured or in respect of any item its sum insured at the time of the loss destruction or damage
        (ii) the sum insured remaining after deduction for any other interruption or interference consequent upon loss destruction or damage occurring during the same period of insurance, unless the Insurer shall have agreed to reinstate any such sum insured

    This policy incorporates the Schedule, Specification and Endorsements which shall be read together as one contract. Words and expressions to which specific meaning is given in any part of this policy shall have the same meaning wherever they appear.

    Signed on behalf of the Insurerer ....

DEFINITION

The words "CONSEQUENTIAL LOSS", in capital letters, shall mean loss resulting from interruption of or interference with the Business carried on by the Insured at the Premises in consequence of loss or destruction of or damage to property used by the Insured at the Premises for the purpose of the Business

APPENDIX I

General Exclusions

This policy does not cover

1 CONSEQUENTIAL LOSS occasioned by riot civil commotion war invasion act of foreign enemy hostilities (whether war be declared or not) civil war rebellion revolution insurrection or military or usurped power

2 loss destruction or damage occasioned by or happening through or occasioning loss or destruction of or damage to any property whatsoever or any loss or expense whatsoever resulting or arising therefrom or any consequential loss directly or indirectly caused by or contributed to by or arising from

   (a) ionising radiations or contamination by radioactivity from any nuclear fuel or from any nuclear waste from the combustion of nuclear fuel
   (b) the radioactive toxic explosive or other hazardous properties of any explosive nuclear assembly or nuclear component thereof

3 CONSEQUENTIAL LOSS in Northern Ireland occasioned by or happening through

   (a) civil commotion
   (b) any unlawful wanton or malicious act committed maliciously by a person or persons acting on behalf of or in connection with any unlawful association

For the purpose of this exclusion

"unlawful association" means any organisation which is engaged in terrorism and includes an organisation which at any relevant time is a proscribed organisation within the meaning of the Northern Ireland (Emergency Provisions) Act 1973

"terrorism" means the use of violence for political ends and includes any use of violence for the purpose of putting the public or any section of the public in fear

In any action suit or other proceedings where the Insurer alleges that by reason of the provisions of this exclusion any CONSEQUENTIAL LOSS is not covered by this policy the burden of proving that such CONSEQUENTIAL LOSS is covered shall be upon the Insured

4 loss resulting from pollution or contamination but this shall not exclude loss resulting from destruction of or damage to property used by the Insured at the Premises for the purpose of the Business, not otherwise excluded, caused by

   (a) pollution or contamination at the Premises which itself results from a peril hereby insured against
   (b) any peril hereby insured against which itself results from pollution or contamination

GENERAL CONDITIONS

1 Policy Voidable

This policy shall be voidable in the event of misrepresentation misdescription or non-disclosure in any material particular.

2 Alteration

This policy shall be avoided if after commencement of this insurance

    (a) the Business be wound up or carried on by a liquidator or receiver or permanently discontinued or

    (b) the interest of the Insured ceases other than by death or

    (c) any alteration be made either in the Business or in the Premises or property therein whereby the risk of loss destruction or damage is increased

unless admitted by the Insurer in writing.

CLAIMS CONDITIONS

1 Action by the Insured

    (a) In the event of any loss destruction or damage in consequence of which a claim is or may be made under this policy the Insured shall

- notify the Insurer immediately
- with due diligence carry out and permit to be taken any action which may reasonably be practicable to minimise or check any interruption of or interference with the Business or to avoid or diminish the loss.

    (b) In the event of a claim being made under this policy the Insured at his own expense shall

- not later than 30 days after the expiry of the Indemnity Period or within such further time as the Insurer may allow, deliver to the Insurer in writing particulars of his claim together with details of all other insurances covering property used by the Insured at the Premises for the purpose of the Business or any part of it or any resulting consequential loss
- deliver to the Insurer such books of account and other business books vouchers invoices balance sheets and other documents proofs information explanation and other evidence as may reasonably be required by the Insurer for the purpose of investigating or verifying the claim together with, if demanded, a statutory declaration of the truth of the claim and of any matters connected with it.

    (c) If the terms of this condition have not been complied with

- no claim under this policy shall be payable and
- any payment on account of the claim already made shall be repaid to the Insurer forthwith.

2 Fraud

If a claim is fraudulent in any respect or if fraudulent means are used by the Insured or by anyone acting on his behalf to obtain any benefit under this policy or if any loss destruction or damage to property used by the Insured at the Premises for the purpose of the Business is caused by the wilful act or with the connivance of the Insured all benefit under this policy shall be forfeited.

3 Contribution

If at the time of any loss destruction or damage resulting in a loss under this policy there be any other insurance effected by or on behalf of the Insured covering such loss or any part of it the liability of the Insurer hereunder shall be limited to its rateable proportion of such loss.

4 Subrogation

Any claimant under this policy shall at the request and expense of the Insurer take and permit to be taken all necessary steps for enforcing rights against any other party in the name of the Insured before or after any payment is made by the Insurer.

5 Arbitration

If any difference arised as to the amount to be paid under this policy (liability being otherwise admitted) such difference shall be referred to an arbitrator to be appointed by the parties in accordance with statutory provisions. Where any difference is by this condition to be referred to arbitration the making of an award shall be a condition precedent to any right of action against the Insurer.

Note: for an insurance relating solely to premises not in the occupation of the Insured the following should be omitted:

the words "used by the Insured" in line 2 (front page), the Definition, General Exclusion 4, Claims Conditions 1(b) and 2 (line 2 only)

the words "for the purpose of the Business" in line 2 (front page), the Definition, General Exclusion 4, Claims Conditions 1(b) and 2

the words "at the Premises" in line 16 (front page)
General Condition 2(c).

THE SCHEDULE

Policy No	
THE INSURER	
THE INSURED	
THE BUSINESS	
THE PREMISES	
ITEMS	As detailed in the attached Specification
TOTAL SPECIFICATION SUM INSURED	£
PERIOD OF INSURANCE	From
	To
RENEWAL DATE	
FIRST PREMIUM	£
ANNUAL PREMIUM	£

THE SPECIFICATION

(This is set out on the basis selected, i.e. Gross Profit, Remuneration/Wages, Revenue, etc.)

APPENDIX II

COMBINED POLICY FOR A TRADE TYPE BUSINESS

It is to be noted that while some abbreviation is effected, in general it is necessary to consider each Section by itself and then read the general provisions to conclude the extent of the cover and the conditions that will operate. See judge's comments in the case *Printpak v A.G.F. Insurance Ltd* [1999]. For example, Section 2 has a material damage proviso despite Section 1 setting out the cover thereto that is given. And the Nuclear exclusion condition variation between material damage and interruption insurance is maintained. This is often not so set out leaving the material damage condition to apply to both sections.

The Interruption Section 2 is on orthodox lines. This can be replaced by other provisions such as the limit being not a stated figure but a percentage of the "stock" amount insured under Section 1, or by a simple statement "not exceeding £....". The return of premium clause may be omitted.

The advantage of the wording set out is that by its conformity to the normal standard wording it can be easily checked to ascertain any abnormal feature. It is, however, not readily understood by a "small business" man, or even a "small" broker.

The other Sections of the policy are not shown here but each will have specific provisions to deal with the cover each provide and if any general conditions are not applicable to a section.

SPECIMEN WORDING

(The Insuer) .... (herein after ....)

(Herein after called the Company) agrees in consideration of payment of the Premium to provide insurance against loss, damage, destruction or liability for injury or damage occurring during the Period of Insurance in accordance with the Policy Sections shown in the schedule subject to the General Conditions of this Policy.

The proposal (which shall mean the signed proposal and declaration and any additional information supplied to the company by or on behalf of the Insured) shall be incorporated in and form the basis of this Policy.

THE SCHEDULE
Policy No: . . . .

First Premium £	Annual Premium £
INSURED	
ADDRESS	
BUSINESS	
PREMISES	

PERIOD OF INSURANCE (both dates inclusive)

(a) From   to
(b) Any subsequent period for which the Company shall have agreed to renew this policy

POLICY SECTIONS

CANCELLING POLICIES

The Policy, the Sections and this Schedule shall be read together as one contract and any word or expression to which a specific meaning has been attached in any part of the Policy, the Sections or this Schedule shall bear such specific meaning wherever it may appear

APPENDIX II

General Conditions

MISDESCRIPTION

1. This Policy shall be voidable in the event of misrepresentation, misdescription, or non-disclosure in any material particular.

ALTERATION

2. This Policy shall be avoided with respect to any item thereof in regard to which there be any alteration after the commencement of this insurance
   (i) by removal or
   (ii) whereby the risk of loss or damage is increased or
   (iii) whereby the insured's interest ceases by will or operation of law, unless such alteration be admitted by memorandum signed by or on behalf of the Company.

EXCLUSIONS

3. This Policy does not cover
   (i) loss or damage occasioned by or in consequence of or arising out of war, invasion, act of foreign enemy, hostilities (whether war be declared or nor), civil war, rebellion, revolution, insurrection or military or usurped power, earthquake, subterranean fire, riot and civil commotion.
   (ii) except in respect of claims arising under Employers Liability or Personal Accident sections loss or destruction of or damage to any property whatsoever or any loss or expense whatsoever resulting or arising therefrom or any consequential loss or any legal liability expense whatsoever resulting or arising therefrom or any consequential loss or damage to any property of whatsoever nature, directly or indirectly caused by or contributed to by or arising from
       (a) ionising radiations or contamination by radioactivity from any nuclear fuel or from any nuclear fuel or from any nuclear waste from the combustion of nuclear fuel
       (b) the radioactive toxic explosive or other hazardous properties of any explosive nuclear assembly or nuclear component thereof.

CLAIMS

4. On the happening of any loss or damage or event likely to give rise to a claim under this Policy the Insured shall forthwith give notice thereof in writing to the Company and shall within 30 days after such loss or damage, or such further time as the Company may in writing allow, at his own expense deliver to the Company a claim in writing containing as particular an account as may be reasonably practicable of the several articles or

portions of property lost or damaged and of the amount of loss or damage thereto respectively having regard to their value at the time of the loss or damage together with details of any other insurances on any property hereby insured. The Insured shall also give to the Company all such proofs and information with respect to the claim as may reasonably be required together with (if demanded) a statutory declaration of the truth of the claim and of any matters connected therewith. No claim under this Policy shall be payable unless the terms of this condition have been complied with.

FRAUD

5. If a claim be in any respect fraudulent or if any fraudulent means or devices be used by the Insured or anyone acting on his behalf to obtain any benefit under this Policy or if any loss or damage be occasioned by the wilful act or with the connivance of the Insured all benefit under this Policy shall be forfeited.

REINSTATEMENT

6. If the Company elect or become bound to reinstate or replace any property the Insured shall at his own expense produce and give to the Company all such plans, documents, books, and information as the Company may reasonably require. The Company shall not be bound to reinstate exactly or completely, but only as circumstances permit and in reasonably sufficient manner and shall not in any case be bound to expend in respect of any one of the items insured more than the sum insured thereon.

RIGHT OF ENTRY AND SALVAGE

7. On the happening of any destruction or damage in respect of which a claim is or may be made under this Policy the Company and every person authorised by the Company may, without thereby incurring any liability, and without diminishing the right of the Company to rely upon any conditions of this Policy enter, take or keep possession of the building or premises where the destruction or damage has happened, and may take possession of or require to be delivered to them any of the property hereby insured and may keep possession of and deal with such property for all reasonable purposes and in any reasonable manner. This condition shall be evidence of the leave and licence of the Insured to the Company so to do. If the Insured or anyone acting on his behalf shall not comply with the requirements of the Company or shall hinder or obstruct the Company in doing any of the above-mentioned acts then all benefit under this Policy shall be forfeited. The Insured shall not in any case be entitled to abandon any property to the Company whether taken possession of by the Company or not.

CONTRIBUTION AND AVERAGE

8   If at the time of any loss of or damage to any property hereby insured there be any other insurance effected by or on behalf of the Insured covering any of the property lost or damaged, the liability of the Company hereunder shall be limited to its rateable proportion of such loss or damage.

If any such other insurance shall be subject to any Condition of Average this Policy, if not already subject to any Condition of Average, shall be subject to Average in like manner.

If any other insurance effected by or on behalf of the Insured is expressed to cover any of the property hereby insured, but is subject to any provision whereby it is excluded from ranking concurrently with this Policy either in whole or in part or from contributing rateably to the destruction or damage, the liability of the Company hereunder shall be limited to such proportion of the destruction or damage as the sum hereby insured bears to the value of the property.

SUBROGATION

9.   Any claimant under this Policy shall at the request and at the expense of the Company do and concur in doing and permit to be done all such acts and things as may be necessary or reasonably required by the Company for the purpose of enforcing any rights and remedies, or of obtaining relief or indemnity from other parties to which the Company shall be or would become entitled or subrogated upon its paying for or making good any loss or damage under this Policy, whether such acts and things shall be or become necessary or required before or after his indemnification by the Company.

CANCELLATION

10.   The Company shall not be bound to accept any renewal of this Policy, and may at any time give thirty days' notice to the Insured to cancel this Policy and thereupon the Insured shall be entitled to the return of a proportionate part of the last premium paid in respect of the unexpired term of the Policy. This termination shall be without prejudice to any rights or claims of the Insured or the Company prior to the expiration of such notice.

PROCEEDINGS

11.   The Insured shall not, except at his own cost, negotiate, pay, settle, admit or repudiate any claim without the written consent of the Company. The Company shall be entitled to undertake, in the name and on behalf of the Insured, the absolute conduct and control of any proceedings and any settlement of the same. The Insured shall render to the Company all

necessary information and assistance to enable the Company to settle or resist any claim or to institute proceedings.

WARRANTIES

12. Every Warranty to which the property insured or any item thereof is, or may be, made subject, shall from the time the Warranty attaches apply and continue to be in force during the whole currency of this Policy, and non-compliance with any such Warranty, whether it increases the risk or not, shall be a bar to any claim in respect of such property or item; provided that whenever this Policy is renewed a claim in respect of destruction or damage occurring during the renewal period shall not be barred by reason of a Warranty not having been complied with at any time before the commencement of such period.

ARBITRATION

13. If any difference shall arise as to the amount to be paid under this Policy (liability being otherwise admitted) such difference shall be referred to an arbitrator to be appointed by the parties in accordance with the Statutory provisions in that behalf for the time being in force. Where any difference is by this condition to be referred to arbitration the making of an award shall be a condition precedent to any right of action against the Company.

CONDITION PRECEDENT

14. It is a condition precedent to any liability on the part of the Company under this Policy that (a) the terms hereof so far as they relate to anything to be done or complied with by the Insured are duly and faithfully observed and fulfilled by the Insured and by any other person who may be entitled to be indemnified under this Policy (b) the statements made and the answers given in the proposal herein before referred to are true and complete.

NORTHERN IRELAND OVERRIDING EXCLUSION

15. Notwithstanding anything in this Policy or in any extensions thereof, it is hereby declared and agreed that as an exclusion overriding all other terms (including the nature and terms of perils insured against) this Policy does not cover loss or destruction of or damage to any property in Northern Ireland or loss resulting therefrom caused by or happening through or in consequence of:

    (i) civil commotion
    (ii) any unlawful, wanton or malicious act committed maliciously by a person or persons acting on behalf of or in connection with any unlawful association.

NOTE. "Unlawful association" means any organisation which is engaged in terrorism and includes an organisation which at any relevant time is a proscribed organisation within the meaning of the Northern Ireland (Emergency Provisions) Act 1973. "Terrorism" means the use of violence for political ends and includes any use of violence for the purpose of putting the public or any section of the public in fear.

In any action, suit or other proceedings where the Company alleges that by reason of the provisions of this exclusion any loss, destruction or damage is not covered by this Policy the burden of proving that such loss, destruction or damage is covered shall be upon the Insured.

This overriding exclusion applies to this Policy and to any extensions thereof, whether such extensions be issued before or after this overriding exclusion except only if any extension be issued hereafter which expressly cancels this overriding exclusion.

(This Exclusion does not apply to any Liability or Personal Accident Section)

Transfer of Interest

If at the time of destruction or damage to any building hereby insured the Insured shall have contracted to sell his interest in such building and the purchase shall not have been but shall be thereafter completed, the purchaser on the completion of the purchase, if and so far as the property is not otherwise insured by or on behalf of the purchaser against such destruction or damage, shall be entitled to the benefit of this Section so far as it relates to such destruction or damage without prejudice to the rights and liabilities of the Insured or the Company under this Section up to the date of completion.

Supplementary Conditions and Memoranda

1. Extensions Except where specifically insured the buildings and/or contents of small outside buildings, annexes, gangways and conveniences are insured under the respective column headings by the item applying to the building to which such property is attached or belongs.

2. NOTICE The Company must be notified in writing immediately any empty building or empty portion of a building insured hereby becomes occupied and a suitable extra premium paid if required.

3. AVERAGE Whenever a sum insured is declared to be subject to Average, if the property covered thereby shall at the breaking out of any fire or at the commencement of any destruction of or damage to such property by any other peril hereby insured against be collectively of greater value than such sum insured, then the Insured shall be considered as being his own insurer for the difference and shall bear a rateable share of the loss accordingly.

    Exceptions:
    (a) A private dwelling house or household goods and personal effects.
    (b) A building used mainly for public religious worship or for activities in connection therewith.
    (c) Agricultural produce on a farm in Great Britain which will be subject to the Special Condition of Average.
    (d) Any item subject to the Two Conditions of Average.

4. FIRE EXTINGUISHING APPLIANCES Where the Company has agreed to allow a discount for fire extinguishing appliances the Insured warrant that the said appliances will be maintained in efficient working order during the currency of this insurance.

5. RENT The insurance on rent applies only if (any of) the said building(s) or any part thereof is unfit for occupation in consequence of its destruction or damage and then the amount payable shall not exceed such proportion of the sum insured on rent as the period necessary for reinstatement bears to the term of rent insured.

6. ELECTRICAL APPARATUS The Company shall not be liable for damage to or destruction of any electrical plant or apparatus caused by its own over-running, short-circuiting, excessive pressure or self-heating, but should fire extend to and damage or destroy any other part of the plant or apparatus or other property insured hereby, such destruction or damage is not excluded by the Policy.

7. OTHER CONTENTS It is agreed that the term "all other contents" is understood to include in so far as they are not otherwise insured
    (a) Money and stamps (other than national insurance stamps) for an amount not exceeding £500,
    (b) National insurance stamps (including any liability for destruction or damage by fire and any other peril hereby insured against established upon the Insured for such stamps affixed to cards),
    (c) Documents, manuscripts and business books but only for the value of the materials at stationery together with the cost of clerical labour expended in writing up and not for the value to the Insured of the information contained therein,
    (d) Computer systems records, but only for the value of the materials together with the cost of clerical labour and computer time expended in reproducing such records (excluding any expense in connection with the production of information to be recorded therein) and not for the value to the Insured of the information contained therein,
    (e) Patterns, models, moulds, plans and designs for an amount not exceeding the cost of the labour and materials expended in reinstatement,
    (f) Directors', patterns', customers', visitors', and employees pedal cycles tools and other personal effects for an amount not exceeding £500 in respect of any one person.

8. ARCHITECTS', SURVEYORS' AND CONSULTING ENGINEERS' FEES The insurance by each item on buildings and machinery includes an amount in respect of architects', surveyors' and consulting engineers' fees necessarily incurred in the reinstatement of the property insured consequent upon its destruction or damage but not for preparing any claim, it being understood that the amount payable for such destruction or damage and fees shall not exceed in the aggregate the sum insured by each item.

9. PROPERTY TEMPORARILY REMOVED Subject to the following provisions the property insured by this Policy (other than stock in trade or merchandise if insured hereby) is covered whilst temporarily removed for cleaning, renovation, repair or other similar purposes elsewhere on the same or to any other premises and in transit thereto and therefrom by road, rail on inland waterway in Great Britain and Northern Ireland.

The amount recoverable under this extension in respect of each item of the Policy shall not exceed the amount which would have been recoverable had the loss occurred in that part of the premises from which the property is temporarily removed nor in respect of any loss occurring elsewhere than at the said premises 10 % of the sum insured by the item after deducting therefrom the value of any building (exclusive of fixtures and fittings) stock in trade or merchandise insured thereby.

This extension does not apply to property if and so far as it is otherwise insured, nor, as regards losses occurring elsewhere than at the premises from which the property is temporarily removed, to

(a) Motor vehicles and motor chassis
(b) Property held by the Insured in trust other than machinery and plant.

10. REMOVAL OF DEBRIS The insurance by each item of the Policy extends to include costs and expenses necessarily incurred by the Insured with the consent of the Company in

(a) Removing debris,
(b) Dismantling and/or demolishing,
(c) Shoring up or propping, of the portion or portions of the property insured by the said items destroyed or damaged by fire or by any other peril hereby insured against.

The Company will not pay for any costs or expenses:

(1) incurred in removing debris except from the site of such property destroyed or damaged and the area immediately adjacent to such site,
(2) arising from pollution or contamination of property not insured by this Policy.

The liability of the Company under this memorandum and the Policy in respect of any item shall in no case exceed the sum insured thereby.

11. PUBLIC AUTHORITIES The insurance by each item of the Policy applying to "buildings" extends to include such additional cost of reinstatement of the destroyed or damaged property thereby insured as may be incurred solely by reason of the necessity to comply with building or other regulations under or framed in pursuance of any Act of Parliament or with bye-laws of any municipal or local authority provided that

(i) The amount recoverable under this extension shall not include:

(a) The cost incurred in complying with any of the aforesaid regulations or bye-laws

(i) in respect of destruction or damage occurring prior to the granting of this extension.
(ii) in respect of destruction or damage not insured by the Policy.
(iii) under which notice has been served upon the Insured prior to the happening of the destruction or damage.
(iv) in respect of undamaged property or undamaged portions of property, other than foundations (unless foundations are specifically excluded from the insurance by the policy) of that portion of the property destroyed or damaged.

APPENDIX II

(b) The additional cost that would have been required to make good the property damaged or destroyed to a condition equal to its condition when new had the necessity to comply with any of the aforesaid regulations or bye-laws not arisen.

(c) The amount of any rate, tax, duty, development or other charge or assessment arising out of capital appreciation which may be payable in respect of the Property or by the owner thereof by reason of compliance with any of the aforesaid regulations or bye-laws.

(ii) The work of reinstatement must be commenced and carried out with reasonable despatch and in any case must be completed within twelve months after the destruction or damage or within such further time as the Company may (during the said twelve months) in writing allow and may be carried out wholly or partially upon another site (if the aforesaid regulations or bye-laws so necessitate) subject to the liability of the Company under this extension not being thereby increased.

(iii) If the liability of the Company under any item of the Policy apart from this extension shall be reduced by the application of any of the terms and conditions of the Policy then the liability of the Company under this extension in respect of any such item shall be reduced in like proportion.

(iv) The total amount recoverable under any item of the Policy shall not exceed the sum insured thereby.

(v) All the conditions of this Policy except in so far as they may be hereby expressly varied shall apply as if they had been incorporated herein.

12. REINSTATEMENT (N.B. Not applicable to motor vehicles, employees' personal effects and cycles, stock and materials in trade) In the event of the property insured under sums insured marked 'R' of the specification being destroyed or damaged, the basis upon which the amount payable under such sums insured marked 'R' is to be calculated shall be reinstatement of the property destroyed or damaged, subject to the following special provisions and subject also to the terms and conditions of the Policy except in-so-far as the same may be varied hereby.

For the purpose of the insurance under this memorandum "reinstatement" shall mean;

The carrying out of the after mentioned work, namely:

(a) Where property is destroyed, the rebuilding of the property if a building, or, in the case other property, its replacement by similar property, in either case in a condition equal to but not better or more extensive than its condition when new.

(b) Where property is damaged the repair of the damage and the restoration of the damaged portion of the property to a condition substantially the same as but not better or more extensive than its condition when new.

SPECIAL PROVISION

(i) The work of reinstatement (which may be carried out upon another site and in any manner suitable to the requirements of the Insured subject to the liability of the Company not being thereby increased) must be commenced and carried out with reasonable despatch; otherwise no payment beyond the amount which would have been payable under the Policy if this memorandum had not been incorporated therein shall be made.

(ii) When any property insured under this memorandum is damaged or destroyed in part only the liability of the Company shall not exceed the sum representing the cost which the Company could have been called upon to pay for reinstatement if such property had been wholly destroyed.

(iii) No payment beyond the amount which would have been payable under the Policy if this memorandum had not been incorporated therein shall be made until the cost of reinstatement shall have been actually incurred.

(iv) Each item insured under this memorandum is declared to be separately subject to the following Condition of Average, namely:

> If at any time of reinstatement the sum representing 85% of the cost which would have been incurred in reinstatement if the whole of the property covered by such item had been destroyed exceeds the sum insured thereon at the breaking out of any fire or at the commencement of any destruction of or damage to such property by any other peril hereby insured against, then the Insured shall be considered as being his own insurer for the difference between the sum insured and the sum representing the cost of reinstatement of the whole of the property and shall bear a rateable proportion of the loss accordingly.

(v) No payment beyond the amount which would have been payable under the Policy if this memorandum had not been incorporated therein shall be made if at the time of any destruction or damage to any property insured hereunder such property shall be covered by any other insurance effected by or on behalf of the Insured which is not upon the identical basis of reinstatement set forth herein.

(vi) Where by reason of any of the above special provisions no payment is to be made beyond the amount which would have been payable under the Policy if this memorandum had not been incorporated therein the rights and liabilities of the Company and the Insured in respect of the destruction of damage shall be subject to the terms and conditions of the Policy, including any condition of Average therein, as if this memorandum had not been incorporated therein.

APPENDIX II

13. FIREPROOF DOORS AND SHUTTERS Warranted that all fireproof doors and shutters will be kept closed except during working hours and will be maintained in efficient working order.

14. REPAIRS AND ALTERATIONS Joiners and other tradesman may be employed to effect repairs or minor structural alterations in all or any of the buildings insured without prejudice to the insurance hereby.

15. REINSTATEMENT OF SUM INSURED AFTER LOSS In the event of loss the sum insured by this Policy will be automatically reinstated from the date of the loss unless written notice is given to the contrary either by the Company or by the Insured and the Insured undertake to pay such necessary premiums as may be required for such reinstatement from that date.

16. COAL Where coal and/or coke is insured by this Policy destruction or damage caused by its own spontaneous heating or combustion is covered notwithstanding anything in the Policy contained to the contrary.

17. DESIGNATION For the purpose of determining where necessary the column or heading under which any property is insured, it is agreed to accept the designation under which such property has been entered in the insured's books.

18. DOCUMENTS TEMPORARILY REMOVED Notwithstanding anything contained herein to the contrary the insurance by this Policy applying wholly or partly to deeds and other documents (including stamps thereon), manuscripts, plans and writing of every description and books (written and printed) extends to cover such property for an amount not exceeding 10% of the value thereof whilst temporarily removed to any other premises not in the Insured's occupation and whilst in transit by road, rail or inland waterway all in Great Britain and Northern Ireland.

WARRANTIES

Warranted that

1. Any combustible trade waste including oily and/or greasy wipes, cloths and swarf which remains in the buildings overnight be kept in metal receptacles having metal lids.

2. No liquids, solutions or paints having a flash point closed cup below 32°C (90°F) -

    (i) applied otherwise than in accordance with the A.B.I. Recommendations in connection with Spraying and other Painting Processes involving the use of Highly Flammable Liquids or the Recommendations for the use of Portable Electrostatic Spray Painting Equipment

    (ii) stored in excess of 50 litres

3. Working in wood (other than for maintenance) by fixed power-operated machines be not done.

4. No processing of plastics be done.

5. No unattended testing be done.

MEMORANDA

1. The insurance is subject to the attached printed Supplementary Conditions and Memoranda, but paragraphs 8 and/or 10 shall not apply where architects', surveyors' and consulting engineers' fees and/or removal of debris are insured by a separate item on this specification.

2. The insurance by each item of this policy (other than any item applying solely to fees, rent, removal of debris or private dwelling houses) is declared to be separately subject to Average as set out in Paragraph 3 of the attached Supplementary Conditions and Memoranda.

3. The insurance includes the additional perils specified in the attached Special Perils Extension.

SECTION 1

FIRE

The Company agrees (subject to the conditions contained herein or endorsed or otherwise expressed hereon which conditions shall so far as the nature of them respectively will permit be deemed to be conditions precedent to the right of the Insured to recover hereunder) that in the event of the following property insured being destroyed or damaged by:

(1) Fire (whether resulting from explosion or otherwise) not occasioned by or happening through its own spontaneous fermentation or heating or its undergoing any process involving the application of heat;

(2) Lightning;

(3) Explosion, not occasioned by or happening through any of the perils referred to in General Condition No.3
   (i) of boilers used for domestic purposes only;
   (ii) in a building not being part of any gas works, of gas used for domestic purposes or used for lighting or heating the building

The Company will pay to the Insured the value of the property at the time of the happening of its destruction or the amount of such damage or at is option reinstate or replace such property or any part thereof;

Provided that the liability of the Company shall in no case exceed in respect of each item the sum expressed to be insured thereon or in the whole the total sum insured hereby, or such other sum or sums as may be substituted therefor by memorandum hereon or attached hereto signed by or on behalf of the Company;

On property as more particularly described in the attached specification which is deemed to be incorporated in and to form part of this Section but not exceeding the total sum insured stated in the said specification;

Except as otherwise stated the buildings described herein are built of brick, stone or concrete and roofed with slates, tiles, metal, concrete, asphalt or sheets or slabs composed entirely of incombustible mineral ingredients.

EXCLUSIONS

This Section does not cover:

(a) Destruction or damage by explosion (whether the explosion be occasioned by fire or otherwise) } except as stated on the face hereof.

(b) Goods held in trust or on commission, money, securities, stamps, documents, manuscripts, business books, computer systems records, patterns, models, moulds, plans, designs, explosives } unless specially mentioned as insured by this Section.

(c) Destruction of or damage to property which, at the time of the happening of such destruction or damage, is insured by, or would, but for the existence of this Section, be insured by any marine policy or policies, except in respect of any excess beyond the amount which would have been payable under the marine policy or policies had this insurance not been effected.

(d) Loss or destruction or damage caused by pollution or contamination except (unless otherwise excluded) destruction of or damage to the property insured caused by

  (i) pollution or contamination which itself results from a peril hereby insured against

  (ii) any peril hereby insured against which itself results from pollution or contamination.

APPENDIX II

SPECIFICATION REFERRED TO IN SECTION 1 OF POLICY NO.

PROPERTY INSURED   SUM INSURED
                                                                                         £

1.   The buildings(s) including landlord's fixtures and fittings therein and thereon, situate and occupied as stated.

     Except as otherwise stated the undernoted buildings are:

     (a)   brick, stone or concrete built and roofed with slates, tiles, metal, concrete, asphalt or slabs or sheets composed entirely of incombustible mineral ingredients.

     (b)   occupied solely by the Insured.

SITUATION

OCCUPATION

2.   Machinery, plant and all other contents, the property of the Insured or held by them/him in trust for which they are/he is responsible (excluding landlord's fixtures and fittings, stock and materials in trade and property more specifically insured) therein and thereon.

3.   Stock and materials in trade the property of the Insured or held by them/him in trust or on commission for which they are/he is responsible therein.

                                              TOTAL SUM INSURED

SPECIAL PERILS EXTENSION

The insurance by this section shall, subject to the Special Conditions overleaf, extend to include destruction or damage (by fire or otherwise) of or to the property insured directly caused by such of the undernoted perils as are enumerated below:

ITEMS (as set down)	PERILS INSURED (as set down)

1A STORM or TEMPEST excluding

    (a) Destruction or damage by:

        (i) the escape of water from the normal confines of any natural or artificial water course (other than water tanks, apparatus or pipes) or lake, reservoir, canal or dam

        (ii) inundation from the sea whether resulting from storm or tempest or otherwise

    (b) Destruction or damage attributable solely to change in the water table level

    (c) Destruction or damage by frost, subsidence or landslip

    (d) Destruction or damage to fences and gates, and movable property in the open

    (e) The first £ of each and every loss after the application of the condition of average. Where the insurance applies to two or more separate premises the exclusion shall apply to each premises separately.

1B STORM, TEMPEST or FLOOD excluding

    (a) Destruction or damage attributable solely to change in the water table level

    (b) Destruction or damage by frost, subsidence or landslip

    (c) Destruction or damage to fences and gates and movable property in the open

    (d) The first £ of each and every loss after the application of the condition of average. Where the insurance applies to two or more separate premises the exclusion shall apply to each premises separately.

2 BURSTING or OVERFLOWING of WATER TANKS, APPARATUS OR PIPES excluding

    (a) Destruction or damage by water discharged or leaking from an installation of automatic sprinklers

    (b) The first £ of each and every loss after the application of the condition of average. Where the insurance applies to two or more separate premises the exclusion shall apply to each premises separately.

[OR USING A MORE MODERN WORDING]

2 ESCAPE OF WATER
DAMAGE caused by ESCAPE OF WATER FROM ANY TANK APPARATUS OR PIPE excluding

(a) DAMAGE by water discharged or leaking from any automatic sprinkler installation

(b) DAMAGE in respect of any building which is empty or not in use

(c) the first £ of each and every loss in respect of each separate premises as ascertained after the application of any condition of average (under insurance).
Where the insurance applies to two or more separate premises the exclusion shall apply to each premises separately.

3A RIOT, CIVIL COMMOTION, STRIKERS, LOCKED-OUT WORKERS or persons taking part in LABOUR DISTURBANCES or MALICIOUS PERSONS ACTING on behalf of or in connection with any POLITICAL ORGANISATION, excluding

(a) Loss or damage occasioned by or happening through confiscation or destruction or requisition by order of the government or any public authority

(b) Loss or damage resulting from cessation of work

(c) Loss or damage in Ireland or Northern Ireland

N.B. On the happening of any loss, destruction or damage under paragraph 3A full details of such loss, destruction or damage shall be furnished to the Company within seven days.

3B RIOT, CIVIL COMMOTION, STRIKERS, LOCKED-OUT WORKERS or persons taking part in LABOUR DISTURBANCES or MALICIOUS PERSONS excluding

(a) Loss or damage occasioned by or happening through confiscation or destruction or requisition by order of the government or any public authority

(b) Loss or damage resulting from cessation of work

(c) As regards destruction or damage (other than by fire or explosion) directly caused by malicious persons not acting on behalf of or in connection with any political organisation
    (i) destruction or damage by theft

(ii) the first £ of each and every loss as ascertained after the application of any condition of average

(d) Loss or damage in Ireland or Northern Ireland

N.B. 1. In so far as this insurance relates to destruction or damage (other than by fire or explosion) directly caused by malicious persons, it is a condition precedent to any claim, that immediate notice of the destruction or damage shall have been given by the Insured to the police authority.

N.B. 2. On the happening of any loss, destruction or damage under paragraph 3B full details of such loss, destruction or damage shall be furnished to the Company within seven days.

4 EXPLOSION excluding

(a) destruction or damage by explosion (other than destruction or damage by fire resulting from explosion) occasioned by the bursting of a boiler (not being a boiler used for domestic purposes only), economiser or other vessel, machine or apparatus in which internal pressure is due to steam only and belonging to or under the control of the Insured

(b) damage to or destruction of vessels, machinery or apparatus or their contents, resulting from the explosion thereof

N.B. For the purpose of this insurance pressure waves caused by aircraft and other aircraft and other aerial devices travelling at sonic or supersonic speeds shall not be deemed explosion.

5 AIRCRAFT AND OTHER AERIAL DEVICES or articles dropped therefrom, excluding destruction or damage occasioned by pressure waves caused by aircraft and other aerial devices travelling at sonic or supersonic speeds.

6A IMPACT with the property insured by any road vehicle or animal not belonging to or under the control of the Insured or their employees.

6B IMPACT with the property insured by any road vehicle or animal excluding the first £ of each and every loss after the application of the condition of average caused by any vehicle or animal belonging to or in the custody or control of the Insured or their employees.

7 EARTHQUAKE OR SUBTERRANEAN FIRE.

8 WATER DISCHARGED OR LEAKING FROM THE AUTOMATIC SPRINKLER INSTALLATION(S) IN THE PREMISES provided that such discharge or leakage of water shall be accidental and shall not be occasioned by or happening through:

(a) freezing whilst the premises in the Insured's ownership and/or tenancy are empty or disused

(b) heat caused by fire

(c) explosion (including the blowing up of buildings or blasting), earthquake or subterranean fire.

PROVIDED ALWAYS that all the conditions of the policy (except in so far as they may be hereby expressly varied) shall apply as if they had been incorporated herein.

SPECIAL CONDITIONS

1. Each item of this policy which is subject to any condition or conditions of average is subject to the same condition or conditions under this extension in like manner. The liability of the Insurers under this extension in respect of each other item of the policy shall be limited to the proportion which the sum insured thereunder shall bear to the total insurances effected by or on behalf of the Insured on the same property against ordinary fire loss or damage (i.e. destruction or damage as originally covered by the policy).

2. The liability of the Insurers shall in no case under this extension and the policy exceed the sum insured by each item of the policy.

3. This insurance does not cover

    (a) Destruction or damage directly or indirectly occasioned by or happening through or in consequence of war, invasion, act of foreign enemy, hostilities (whether war be declared or not), civil war, rebellion, revolution, insurrection or military or usurped power, and (if the insurance is not extended to include the perils specified in Paragraph 3A or 3B) riot and civil commotion

    (b) Loss or destruction of or damage to any property whatsoever or any loss or expense whatsoever resulting or arising therefrom directly or indirectly caused by or contributed to by or arising from

        (i) ionising radiations or contamination by radioactivity from any nuclear fuel or from any nuclear waste from the combustion of nuclear fuel

        (ii) the radioactive, toxic, explosive or other hazardous properties of any explosive nuclear assembly or nuclear component thereof

    (c) Loss or destruction or damage caused by pollution or contamination except (unless otherwise excluded) destruction of or damage to the property insured caused by

        (i) pollution or contamination which itself results from a peril hereby insured against

        (ii) any peril hereby insured against which itself results from pollution or contamination

    (d) Consequential loss or damage of any kind or description (other than rent if insured)

(e) Loss or destruction of or damage to any property in Northern Ireland or loss resulting therefrom caused by or happening through or in consequence of:

    (i) civil commotion

    (ii) any unlawful, wanton or malicious act committed maliciously by a person or persons acting on behalf of or in connection with any unlawful association

For the purpose of this condition:

> "Unlawful Association" means any organisation which is engaged in terrorism and includes an organisation which at any relevant time is a proscribed organisation within the meaning of the Northern Ireland (Emergency Provisions) Act, 1973.

> "Terrorism" means the use of violence for political ends and includes any use of violence for the purpose of putting the public or any section of the public in fear.

In any action, suit or other proceedings where the Insurers allege that by reason of the provisions of this condition any loss, destruction or damage is not covered by this policy the burden of proving that such loss, destruction or damage is covered shall be upon the Insured.

(f) Damage to automatic sprinkler installation(s) other than that caused by water accidentally discharged or leaking from the installation(s).

4. In so far as this insurance relates to destruction or damage by water discharged or leaking from automatic sprinkler installation(s) in the premises

    (a) The Insured shall take all reasonable steps to prevent frost and other damage to the automatic sprinkler installation(s) and, so far as his responsibility extends, to maintain the installation(s) including the automatic external alarm signal in efficient condition. In the event of any discharge or leakage from the said installation(s), the Insured shall do and permit to be done all things practicable, whether by removal or otherwise, to save and protect the property insured

    (b) When any changes, repairs or alterations to the automatic sprinkler installation(s) are proposed written notice thereof is to be given to the Insurers, and their agreement obtained in writing.

5. The Insurers shall have access to the premises at all reasonable times for purposes of inspection and if the Insurers notify the Insured of defects in the construction or condition of the automatic sprinkler installation(s) requiring alteration or repairs the Insurers may also at their option by notice in writing suspend the insurance under this extension until such alterations or repair be made and approved by the Insurers.

SECTION 2

CONSEQUENTIAL LOSS

The Company agrees that if any building or other property or any part thereof used by the Insured at the premises for the purpose of the Business be destroyed or damaged by:

(1) Fire (whether resulting from explosion or otherwise) not occasioned by or happening through

    (a) its own spontaneous fermentation or heating or its undergoing any process involving the application of heat,

    (b) earthquake, subterranean fire, riot, civil commotion, war, invasion, act of foreign enemy, hostilities (whether war be declared or not), civil war, rebellion, insurrection or military or usurped power,

(2) Lightning,

(3) Explosion, not occasioned or happening through any of the perils specified in 1 (b) above,

    (i) of boilers used for domestic purposes only,

    (ii) of any other boilers or economisers on the premises,

    (iii) in a building not being part of any gas works, of gas used for domestic purposes or used for lighting or heating the building,

(destruction or damage so caused being herein after termed Damage) and the business carried on by the Insured at the premises be in consequence thereof interrupted or interfered with

Then the Company will pay to the Insured in respect of each item in the Specification hereto the amount of loss resulting from such interruption or interference in accordance with the provisions therein contained

Provided that at the time of the happening of the damage there shall be in force an insurance covering the interest of the Insured in the property at the premises against such damage and that payment shall have been made or liability admitted therefor under such insurance

And that the liability of the Company shall in no case exceed in respect of each item the sum expressed in the said Specification to be insured thereon or in the whole the total sum insured hereby or such other sum or sums as may hereafter be substituted therefore by memorandum signed by or on behalf of the Company.

INDEMNITY

> The amount which the Insured is entitled to recover under the provisions of the attached specification which is declared to be incorporated in and to form part of this Section but not exceeding the total sum insured and/or estimated gross profit stated in the said specification

SPECIAL CONDITIONS

1. This Section shall be avoided if the business be wound up or carried on by a Liquidator or Receiver or permanently discontinued.

2. This Section does not cover loss resulting from

    (a) Any damage occasioned by or happening through explosion (whether the explosion be occasioned by fire or otherwise) except as stated on the face of this Section

    (b) Pollution or contamination except loss resulting from damage as within defined, not otherwise excluded, caused by

        (i) pollution or contamination at the premises which itself results from damage as within defined

        (ii) damage as within defined which itself results from pollution or contamination.

3. On the happening of any damage in consequence of which a claim is or may be made under this Section, the Insured shall forthwith give notice thereof in writing to the Company and shall with due diligence do and concur in doing and permit to be done all things which may be reasonably practicable to minimise or check any interruption of or interference with the business or to avoid or diminish the loss, and in the event of a claim being made under this Section shall, not later than thirty days after the expiry of the indemnity period or within such further time as the Company may in writing allow, at his own expense deliver to the Company in writing a statement setting forth particulars of his claim, together with details of all other insurances covering the damage or any part of it or consequential loss of any kind resulting therefrom. The Insured shall at his own expense also produce and furnish to the Company such books of accounts, and other business books, vouchers, invoices, balance sheets and other documents, proofs, information, explanation and other evidence as may reasonably be required by the Company for the purpose of investigating or verifying the claim together with (if demanded) a statutory declaration of the truth of the claim and of any matters connected therewith. No claim under this Section shall be payable unless the terms of this condition have been complied with and in the event of non-compliance therewith in any respect, any payment on account of the claim already made shall be repaid to the Company forthwith.

4. This Section and the Specification annexed (which forms an integral part of this Policy) shall be read together as one contract and words and expressions to which specific meanings have been attached in any part of this Section or of the Specification shall bear such specific meanings wherever they may appear.

SPECIAL PERILS EXTENSION

The word DAMAGE is extended to include destruction or damage (by fire or otherwise) caused by such of the undernoted perils as are enumerated below:

PERILS INSURED
(as set down)

1A STORM OR TEMPEST excluding

    (a) Destruction or damage by:

        (i) the escape of water from the normal confines of any natural or artificial water course (other than water tanks, apparatus or pipes) or lake, reservoir, canal or dam

        (ii) inundation from the sea whether resulting from storm or tempest or otherwise

    (b) Destruction or damage attributable solely to change in the water table level

    (c) Destruction or damage by frost, subsidence or landslip

    (d) Destruction or damage to fences and gates, and movable property in the open.

1B STORM, TEMPEST OR FLOOD excluding

    (a) Destruction or damage attributable solely to change in the water table level

    (b) Destruction or damage by frost, subsidence or landslip

    (c) Destruction or damage to fences and gates, and movable property in the open.

2 BURSTING OR OVERFLOWING OF WATER TANKS, APPARATUS OR PIPES excluding destruction or damage by water discharged or leaking from an installation of automatic sprinklers.

(See page 81 for an alternative modern wording – ESCAPE OF WATER.)

3A RIOT, CIVIL COMMOTION, STRIKERS, LOCKED-OUT WORKERS or persons taking part in LABOUR DISTURBANCES or MALICIOUS PERSONS acting on behalf of or in connection with any POLITICAL ORGANISATION, excluding

(a) Destruction or damage occasioned by or happening through confiscation or destruction or requisition by order of the government or any public authority.

(b) Destruction or damage resulting from cessation of work

(c) Destruction or damage in Ireland or Northern Ireland

N.B. On the happening of any destruction or damage under Paragraph 3A full details of such destruction or damage shall be furnished to the Company within seven days.

3B RIOT, CIVIL COMMOTION, STRIKERS, LOCKED-OUT WORKERS or persons taking part in LABOUR DISTURBANCES or MALICIOUS PERSONS excluding

(a) Destruction or damage occasioned by or happening through confiscation or destruction or requisition by order of the government or any public authority

(b) Destruction or damage resulting from cessation of work

(c) Destruction or damage in Ireland or Northern Ireland

N.B. On the happening of any loss, destruction or damage under paragraph 3B full details of such destruction or damage shall be furnished to the Company within seven days.

4 EXPLOSION excluding

(a) Loss resulting from destruction or damage by explosion (other than destruction or damage by fire resulting from explosion) occasioned by the bursting of any vessel, machine or apparatus (not being a boiler or economiser on the premises) in which internal pressure is due to steam only and belonging to or under the control of the Insured.

(b) Loss sustained in consequence of the Insured being deprived of the use of any vessel, machine or apparatus (not being a boiler or economiser on the premises) or its contents as a result of the explosion thereof.

N.B. For the purpose of this insurance pressure waves caused by aircraft and other aerial devices travelling at sonic or supersonic speeds shall not be deemed explosion.

APPENDIX II

5   AIRCRAFT AND OTHER AERIAL DEVICES or articles dropped therefrom, excluding destruction or damage occasioned by pressure waves caused by aircraft and other aerial devices travelling at sonic or supersonic speeds.

6   IMPACT by any road vehicle or animal.

7   EARTHQUAKE OR SUBTERRANEAN FIRE.

8   WATER DISCHARGED OR LEAKING FROM THE AUTOMATIC SPRINKLER INSTALLATION(S) IN THE PREMISES provided that such discharge or leakage of water shall be accidental and shall not be occasioned by or happening through:

   (a) Freezing whilst the premises in the Insured's ownership and/or tenancy are empty or disused

   (b) Heat caused by fire

   (c) Explosion (including the blowing up of buildings or blasting), earthquake or subterranean fire

9   THEFT or any attempt thereat involving entry to or exit from the premises by forcible and violent means.

   PROVIDED ALWAYS that all the conditions of the policy (except in so far as they may be hereby expressly varied) shall apply as if they had been incorporated herein.

SPECIAL CONDITION

1   This insurance does not cover

   (a) Loss resulting from destruction or damage directly or indirectly occasioned by or happening through or in consequence of war, invasion, act of foreignenemy, hostilities (whether war be declared or not), civil war rebellion, revolution, insurrection or military or usurped power, and (if the insurance is not extended to include the perils specified in Paragraphs 3A or 3B) riot and civil commotion

   (b) Loss resulting from damage occasioned by or happening through or occasioning - loss or destruction of or damage to any property whatsoever or any loss or expense whatsoever resulting or arising therefrom or any consequential loss directly or indirectly caused by or contributed to by or arising from

      (i) ionising radiations or contamination by radioactivity from any nuclear fuel or from any nuclear waste from the combustion of nuclear fuel

        (ii) the radioactive, toxic, explosive or other hazardous properties of any explosive nuclear assembly or nuclear component thereof
(c) Loss resulting from damage in Northern Ireland occasioned by or happening through
   (i) civil commotion
   (ii) any unlawful, wanton or malicious act committed maliciously by a person or persons acting on behalf of or in connection with any unlawful association.

   For the purpose of this condition:

   "Unlawful Association" means any organisation which is engaged in terrorism and includes an organisation which at any relevant time is a proscribed organisation within the meaning of the Northern Ireland (Emergency Provisions) Act, 1973.

   "Terrorism" means the use of violence for political ends and includes any use of violence for the purpose of putting the public or any section of the public in fear.

   In any action, suit or other proceedings where the Insurers allege that by reason of the provisions of this condition any loss, resulting from such damage is not covered by this policy the burden of proving that such loss, destruction or damage is covered shall be upon the Insured.

(d) Loss resulting from pollution or contamination except loss resulting from damage as within defined, not otherwise excluded, caused by
   (i) pollution or contamination at the premises which itself results from damage as within defined
   (ii) damage as within defined which itself results from pollution or contamination.

APPENDIX II

SPECIFICATION REFERRED TO IN SECTION 2 OF POLICY NO AND FORMING AN INTEGRAL PART OF THE SCHEDULE THEREIN

Item 1.

ON GROSS PROFIT Sum Insured £ ....

The insurance under this item is limited to loss of gross profit due to (a) REDUCTION IN TURNOVER and (b) INCREASE IN COST OF WORKING and the amount payable as indemnity thereunder shall be:

(a) IN RESPECT OF REDUCTION IN TURNOVER: the sum produced by applying the rate of gross profit to the amount by which the turnover during the indemnity period shall, in consequence of the Damage, fall short of the standard turnover

(b) IN RESPECT OF INCREASE IN COST OF WORKING: the additional expenditure (subject to the provisions of the uninsured working expenses clause) necessarily and reasonably incurred for the sole purpose of avoiding or diminishing the reduction in turnover which but for that expenditure would have taken place during the indemnity period, in consequence of the Damage, but not exceeding the sum produced by applying the rate of gross profit to the amount of the reduction thereby avoided

Less any sum saved during the indemnity period in respect of such of the charges and expenses of the business payable out of gross profit as may cease or be reduced in consequence of the Damage

Provided that if the sum insured by this item be less than the sum produced by applying the rate of gross profit to the annual turnover (or to a proportionately increased multiple thereof where the maximum indemnity period exceeds twelve months) the amount payable shall be proportionately reduced.

DEFINITIONS

NOTE: For the purpose of these definitions any adjustment implemented in current cost accounting shall be disregarded.

INDEMNITY PERIOD: The period beginning with the occurrence of the Damage and ending not later than the maximum indemnity period thereafter during which the results of the business shall be affected in consequence of the Damage.

MAXIMUM INDEMNITY PERIOD: ....months.

TURNOVER: The money paid or payable to the Insured for goods sold and delivered and for services rendered in course of the business at the premises.

GROSS PROFIT: the amount by which:

(i) the sum of the amount of the turnover and the amounts of the closing stock and work in progress

shall exceed

(ii) the sum of the amounts of the opening stock, work in progress and stock purchased and the amount of the uninsured working expenses

NOTE: The amount of the opening and closing stocks and work in progress shall be arrived at in accordance with the Insured's normal accountancy methods, due provision being made for depreciation.

UNINSURED WORKING EXPENSES:

(These to be set out)

Note: The words and expressions used in this definition (other than wages) shall have the meaning usually attached to them in the books and accounts of the Insured.

RATE OF GROSS PROFIT: The rate of gross profit earned on the turnover during the financial year immediately before the date of the damage,

ANNUAL TURNOVER: The turnover during the twelve months immediately before the date of the damage,

STANDARD TURNOVER: The turnover during that period in the twelve months immediately before the date of the damage which corresponds with the indemnity period,

to which such adjustments shall be made as may be necessary to provide for the trend of the business and for variations in or other circumstances affecting the business either before or after the damage or which would have affected the business had the damage not occurred, so that the figures thus adjusted shall represent as nearly as may be reasonably practicable the results which but for the damage would have been obtained during the relative period after the damage.

VALUE ADDED TAX:

To the extent that the Insured is accountable to the tax authorities for Value Added Tax, all terms in this section shall be exclusive of such tax.

ALTERNATIVE TRADING CLAUSE:

If during the indemnity period goods shall be sold or services shall be rendered elsewhere than at the premises for the benefit of the business either by the Insured or by others on his behalf the money paid or payable in respect of such sales or services shall be brought into account in arriving at the turnover during the indemnity period.

UNINSURED WORKING EXPENSES:

If any working expenses of the business be not insured by this section (having been deducted in arriving at the gross profit as defined herein) then in computing the amount recoverable hereunder as increase in cost of working, that proportion only of any additional expenditure shall be brought into account which the gross profit bears to the sum of the gross profit and the uninsured working expenses.

RETURN OF PREMIUM CLAUSE:

In the event of the gross profit (or a proportionately increased multiple thereof where the maximum indemnity period exceeds twelve months) during the financial year most nearly concurrent with any period of insurance as certified by the Insured's auditors being less than the sum insured thereon a pro rata return of premium not exceeding 50% of the premium paid on such sum insured for such period of insurance will be made in respect of the difference. If any damage shall have occurred, giving rise to a claim under this section, such return shall be made in respect only of so much of the said difference as is not due to such Damage.

PROFESSIONAL ACCOUNTANTS CHARGES:

The insurance by Item 1 extends to include the reasonable charges payable by the Insured to his professional accountants/auditors for producing any particulars or details or any other proofs, information or evidence as may be required by the Insurers under the terms of this section and reporting that such particulars or other details are in accordance with the Insured's books of account or other business books or documents provided that the sum of the amount payable under this clause and the amount otherwise payable under this section shall in no case exceed the total sum insured by this section.

DENIAL OF ACCESS EXTENSION:

Subject to the conditions of this section loss resulting from interruption or interference with the business in consequence of Damage (as within defined) to property in the vicinity of the premises destruction of or damage to which shall prevent or hinder the use of the premises or access thereto whether the premises or property of the Insured therein shall be damaged or not shall be deemed to be loss resulting from Damage to property used by the Insured at the premises.

MEMORANDA

1. The insurance includes the additional perils specified in the attached Special Perils Extension.

2. Subject to the conditions of the policy, loss as insured by Item 1 of this policy resulting from interruption of or interference with the business in consequence of damage (as within defined) at the undernoted situations or to property as undernoted shall be deemed to be loss resulting from damage to property used by the Insured at the premises, provided that, after the application of all other terms, conditions and provisions of the policy, the liability under this memorandum in respect of any one occurrence shall not exceed the percentage of the total of the sums insured by Item(s) 1 of the policy, shown below against such situations or property as the limit.

EXTENSION   **LIMIT**

(The premises of the following suppliers then to be listed.)

APPENDIX III

The legal position of the term "Market Practice".

The main source of English Law is the common law of England. This involves the underlying, unwritten law and legal customs of the country.

Although the primary intention has been to apply a uniform system of common law, local customs if recognised are included within the doctrine of common law. They are distinct from those customs within the original framework of common law.

To have legal recognition a local custom requires fulfilment of the following conditions.

- [a] Immemorial existence.
- [b] Continuity.
- [c] Reasonableness.
- [d] Certainty.
- [e] Not disputed.
- [f] Recognised as binding by the persons concerned upon all of them.

Under [a] it has been said that immemorial is from prior to 1189, (the date of legal memory). But it seems that later dates can apply for those customs arising from local activities which have called for them as good commercial business practice, but the universal application is required.

Thus for insurance practice it can be difficult to establish evidence to conform with these legalistic requirements especially after the discontinuance of the "Tariff" insurance authority [F.O.C.], except perhaps for those edicts issued by them previous to their demise [and even here it may be challenged that they are not universally in current practice by the whole market]. The responsibility for the unclear position lies firmly with the Government who created this position, which was often beneficial to the policy-holder.

APPENDIX IV

Disclosure

Some general notes given by the Author in a Report to a High Court

Duty of Disclosure in insurance

1. Insurance policies fall within the class of contracts which are subject to the principle *"Uberrimae fides"* and from this stems the duty of disclosure.

Disclosure involves the question of materiality of the information concerned and this will depend on (a) the class of insurance that is being underwritten and (b) whether it is direct insurance or re-insurance.

Originally in English Law, the principles of "Utmost good faith" and "disclosure" developed from the practice of "Marine Insurance", by case law subsequently codified in the Marine Insurance Act 1906. It has however to be remembered that there are some aspects of marine insurance which are specific to it and not applicable to other classes either at all or are modified. For example "Sue and Labour" and the non essential nature of the original insured in cargo insurance which can be transferred without prior approval of the insurer.

The underwriting of insurance is neither a science nor an art form, it involves both in the sense of statistical analysis of past experience as science and judgement of proposers and commercial establishments as a matter of art but additionally must be added "feel" which incorporates the economic, social, geographic and future in all these spheres against the past.

Thus for a direct insurance, whether through a broker or not, the Underwriter will seek via a proposal form or questionnaire:

    (a) That statistical data which he can then consider, compare and make judgement from against his records etc.
    (b) That general information of the specific proposer, his business and activities to the extent that they will add to his own statistics or amplify his appreciation of that which he is underwriting.

He has to work in an orderly commercially administrative fashion that will provide a consistent and coherent programme allowing him to assess his practice and yet not seek to be unable to match his competitors in speed or be unrealistic in the detail he needs.

His underwriting basis while relying on that which is material to the risk is NOT

    (a) Everything he would like to know as this would overwhelm his recording system and prevent proper statistical analysis to be made, or
    (b) Everything which an outsider or a theoretical approach would consider ought to be considered by him.

For example:

    [i]   private house insurance does give rating consideration to the nature of the roof covering and this needs to be disclosed. The construction of the roof itself, wood or concrete, etc. or even the underlying of the tiles by asphalt felting or if there is roof insulation, are not matters which an underwriter wishes disclosed as they do not affect his assessment of the risk or the rate he will charge.

    [ii]   an industrial plant may use machinery for its production. If these are wood working machines exact detail is required of the number and usage/type as this will affect the rating etc. If the machines are metal working the number and type/usage is not material to the rating.

    [iii]   in motor insurance age of drivers by age bands is a normal rating/acceptance feature, in theft cases postal district coding frequently used to vary rates, but neither of these would be material to the fire insurer of a property as such.

2. The judgement of nondisclosure is made on what is termed the view of a prudent insurer and not the actual insurer himself. The term "prudent" as used in the 18th Century meaning implied a man of business acomen, Thus it is the practice of underwriters of standing and experience in the class of insurance that can assist to establish what is material in a case of difference.
(This needs to be reviewed against the *Pan Atlantic v Pine Top* [1994] rulings).

3. The current general industrial insurance market includes large insurance groups operating on an international basis but with Headquarters based in one of four or five countries and it is normal for them to be the insurers of the large counterpart national or multi-national business corporations. They can deal with the geographical aspects and the size of exposures within large cases by assistance from other major insurers. The placings are frequently handled by a so called "mega" broker and it is normal for the Insured to have his own insurance department which these days would be most likely to be within the Risk Management Department. Thus the parties to the arrangements will be known to each other in the form indicated.

4. The practical aspect of the placing and disclosure are thus well known to these parties and frequently the matter is changed by the insurer himself taking on a direct role of ascertaining the risk features by sending his own Surveyor to the insured premises.

5. The duty of disclosure also involves seven factors that apply;

    (a)   The material information must be known to the Insured and not to the Insurer, I omit the aspects of the intermediary as in this case I am instructed that no point so arises.

This raises a major question of, 'Who is the Insured?' At law a public company operates through a very narrow channel but is that the limitation to be applied to who needs to know and thus from whom was the disclosure not supplied?

I believe that in English law and in English insurance practice the disclosure is not a matter of the formal Board of the Company nor its Secretary, (although withholding by them of information that is material might in some circumstances be material and applicable to consideration), but the effective managers of the business and any colleague whose role is to be responsible for the onward advice to insurers.

In this case, as in many others of a similar organisation, I believe that the fact that the Risk Manager is involved with the insurer with the knowledge of each of their positions, then the duty of disclosure of what the Insured knows is in fact what the Risk Manager knows, coupled only with the special situation if management falsely, or deliberately, held back from him material information or misrepresented it. These two exceptional situations are normally catered for by the policy exclusion of fraud or misrepresentation and are not in contemplation here.

Thus, as would happen also in a small business, the non-knowledge by the Insured by mistake, or worse, from his employees of material information is not a matter of non disclosure under the policy, by him the Insured. In an international company and in those with many sites etc. the practicality of disclosure on a wider basis is known by insurers as not possible, and in my view, even if it existed as a technical legal requirement, and I do not believe that it does, their knowledge is such that they have waived seeking more than that which they actually ask at any relevant time.

(b) What knowledge has the Insurer and this includes that which he should have in his general activity, in being an insurer of that class of business? He knows that a Butcher in his shop uses knives and it is not non disclosure if the Butcher does not mention this point when proposing for insurance. The inclusion of clauses or the attempt to obviate the clear intention of the contract is not a matter acceptable to the English Courts and they have expressed a view that wilful and malicious behaviour by the Insured is required to fall within any such provision.

(c) Information on which an Insurer is given sufficient to put him on warning to seek more is not a matter of non disclosure, if such further enquiry is not made. Insurers cannot, by neglecting to make use of this information which they have received, or of knowledge which they themselves possess, or in the course of their business should possess, take advantage of their own wilful blindness or negligence, provided that sufficient information so far as the Insured is concerned, has been placed at their disposal.

(d) Facts as to which the insurers waive information, or as to which the proposer may reasonably infer that the insurers are indifferent, do not comprise non-disclosure.

(e) Facts, the disclosure of which are unnecessary by reason of a policy condition, need not be advised as such.

(f) Matters which do not increase the hazards involved have not to be advised.

(g) All facts of public notoriety are deemed to be known to the insurer.

Misrepresentation in the proposal form

6. This is a matter of fact to be judged on whether the reply is adequate in respect of the materiality to the question asked or put the insurers on sufficient warning for them to seek more information themselves.

Breach of Policy Terms

7. This is a matter of fact to be assessed on what the terms actually require on the face of their statements and whether they are of the nature of:

(a) A warranty (which requires clarity in the terms used that it is to be so read).

(b) A representation as to the current situation (which generally does not mean continued correctness of its statement for the future), or

(c) A policy condition and this may not necessarily be a warranty.

TABLE OF LAW CASES

Aluminium Wire & Cable & Allstate Insce Co Ltd [1958]
2 Lloyd's Rep. 280
Banque Keyser Ullman v Scandia Insce [1987]
2 WLR 1300: 1L1 L Rep 69
and sub to House of Lords
Bates v Hewitt [1867] L.R. 2 QB 595; 36 L.J.Q.B. 282;
15 W.R. 1172.
Baxendale v Harvey [1859] 4 H&N 445; 28 L.J.Ex 236;
33 L.T. [o.s.] 110; 7 W.R. 494
Beauchamp v National Mutual Indemnity Ins Co [1937]
2 All E.R. 19
Beresford v Royal Insc Co [1938]
A.C. 586; 107 L.J.K.B. 464; 158 L.T. 459; 54 T.L.R. 789; 82 S.J. 431;
2 K.B. 197
Booth [Henry] & Sons v Commercial Union [1923]
14 L1. L.R. 114 29 Digest [Repl]
486
Brandon Electrical Engineering Co v William Press and Sons
[1956] 106 L.J.B. 332
British Celanese Ltd v A H Hunt [Capacitors] Ltd [1969]
2 All ER 1252; [1969] W.L.R. 959; 113 Sol.Jo. 368
Britton v Royal [1866] 4 F&F 905; 15 L.T. 72; 29 Digest
[Repl] 446
Caltex Oil (Australia) Pty Ltd v The Dredger "Willemsted" [1977]
A.L.R. 227
Carter v Boehm [1766] 3 Burr 1905; 1 Wm Bl 593; 29 Digest
[Rep1] 43
City Tailors v Evans [1921] 91 L.J.K.B. 379; 126 L.T. 439;
38 T.L.R. 230; [1921] All E.R. 399; 9. L1. L.R. 46
C.A.; 29 Digest [Rep1] 485
Constantirou v Aegen Ins Co, and Stevenson Prvte (1995)
C.T.I. v Oceanus [1984] 1 L1 Rep. 476 C.A.; reversing
[1982] 2 L1 Rep 178; [1982]
Com. L.R. 68.
Dalziel [Airdrie] Ltd v Burgh of Airdrie [1966] S.L.T.
[Sh.Ct.] 39
Elcock v Thomas [1949] 2 All E.R. 381; [1949] 2 K.B.
755; 65 T.L.R. 566; Sol. Jo. 562; 82 L1.L
Rep.892; 29 Digest [Rep1] 486
Electrocrome Ltd v Welsh Plastics Ltd [1968]
2 All E.R. 205; Digest Supp
Elliott v Sir Robert McAlpine & Sons Ltd [1966]
2 L1 Rep 482

Forsiherings Vesta v Butcher [1986] 2 All E.R. 488; [1986] 2 Lloyd's Rep. 179
Fraser v Furman, Miller Smith & Partners Third Party [1967]
    1 W.L.R. 898; 111 S.J. 471; [1967] 3 All E.R. 57;
    2 K.I.R. 483; [1967] 2 Ll Rep 1
Glengate - K G Properties v Norwich Union Fire [1994]
    Appeal upheld Judge Phillips J at first instance by two
    Judges decision against one dissenting ref C.A. QBCM
    F94/1121/B [1995] and subsequently appeal to the House of Lords refused
Hedley Byrne & Co v Heller & Partners [1964] A.C. 465; [1963] 3 W.L.R. 101;
    107 S.J. 454; [1963] 2 All E.R. 575; [1963] 1 Ll Rep 485; 234 L.T. 381; 67
    Accountant's Mag 518; 107 S.J. 582, 622; 113 L.J. 779; 114 L.J. 202, 209; 74
    Accty 877; 149 Acct 520; 60 L.S. Gaz 740; 80 S.A.L.J. 482; 27 M.L.R. 121;
    [1964] J.B.L. 231; 98 I.L.T. 215; 3 Osgoode Hall L.J. 89; 5 Chart. Sec. 19; 74
    Yale L.J. 286; 153 Acct 16; 76 Accty 829, [1972] J.B.L. 27 [H.L.] affirming
    [1962] 1.Q.B. 396; [1961] 3 W.L.R. 1225; 105 S.J. 910; [1961] 3 All E.R. 891;
    [25 M.L.R. 246; 105 S.J. 1075; 78 L.Q.R. 107]; [1961] C.L.Y. 518, C.A.;
    affirming The Times Dec 21 1960; [1960] C.L.Y. 186; [45 A.L. 20. J. 20]
Irving v Manning [1847] 1.H.L. Cas 287; 6 C.B. 391; 6 L.T. 108; 10.L.T. 877; 29
    Digest [Rep1] 314
Le Banque Financiere v Westgate Insce [1986].
Lloyd J.J. Instruments v Northern Star Insce Co [1957] called the Miss J.J. case. 1
    Lloyds Rep 32
Mackenzie v Coulson [1869] L.R. 8 Eq. 368
McDonnell v Beacon Fire [1857] 7 U.C.C.P. 308
Mathie v Argonaut Marine [1925] 21 Ll.L.R. 145
Mutual Life of New York v Ontario Metal Products [1925]
    A.C. 344; 94 L.J.P.C. 60; 132 L.T. 652; 41 T.L.R. 183
Pan Atlantic v Pine Top [1994] House of Lords W.L.R.
    12.8.94. dismissed appeal from Ct of Appeal [1993]
    1 Ll Rep 496 who had dismissed plaintiff's appeal from Waller J [1992]
    1 Ll Rep 101 Over ruling in part C.T.I. v Oceanus
Pawsey v Scotland Union and National Insce (1906)
Polikoff v North British [1936] 55 Ll. L.R. 279
Printpak v A.G.F. Insurance Ltd [1999] – The Times 3/2/99
Rayner v Preston [1881]. 18 Ch D 1; 50 L.J.Ch 472; 44
    L.T. 787; 45 J.P. 829; 29 W.R. 547
Reynolds and Anderson v Phoenix Assce [1978] 2 Ll Rep 440
Rowlands [Mark] Ltd v Berni Inns Ltd [1986] 1 Q.B. 211; [1985] 3 W.L.R. 964;
    129 S.J. 811; [1986] 3 All E.R. 473; [1985] 276 E.G. 191; 2 Lloyds Rep 437;
    135 New L.J. 962; [1986] 83 L.S. Gaz 35; C.A. affirming [1984] New L.J. 236
Rozanes v Bowen [1928] 32 Ll Rep 98 aff. [1928] 31 Ll Rep 231
Schoolman v Hall [1951] 1 Ll Rep 139
SCM [U.K.] Ltd v W & J Whittall & Sons Ltd [1970]
    16.7.70 Ct of Appeal 1971 1 Q.B. 337

Stanley v Western Insc Co [1868] L.R. 3 Ex 71; 37 L.J. Ex 73; 17 L.T. 513; 16 W.R. 369

Stavrous Constantinou v Aegon Insce Co [UK] Ltd & Others [1995]

Thompson v Hopper [1856] 6 E.B. 172; 25 L.J.Q.B. 240; 26 L.T. [os] 308; 2 Jur [ns] 608; 4 W.R.360

W.&J. Lane v Spratt [1970] 2 Q.B. 480; [1969] 3 W.L.R. 950; 113 S.J. 920; [1970] 1 All E.R. 162; 2 Lloyds Rep 229

Woodfall & Rimmer v Moyle [1942] 1 K.B. 66; 111 L.J.K.B. 122; 166 L.T. 49; 58 T.L.R. 28; 86 S.J. 63; [1941] All E.R. 304; 71 Ll L.R. 15

INDEX

Accountancy aspects	4	M2K	45
Accumulated stocks	7	Millennium bug	45
Additional Expenditure	19	Minimisation of loss	7
Aggravation of loss	12	Mining	30, 31
Agreed loss basis	1, 2, 3, 23		
Alteration of Risk	39, 44	Non Disclosure	33, 34, 35
Auditors cover	2		
		Onus of proof	2
Car Parks	30	Other circumstances	3, 12, 13
Change in participation of insurers	41	Outside events	3, 5
Combined policy	36		
Consequential loss	22	Payments on account	18, 21, 22
Contribution rent covers	43	Premises	29, 30
Cotton industry	14	Production changes	12
Criminal offence disclosure of	37	Public Authorities	7
Customer loss	8		
		Rate of Gross Profit	20
Delays by others	14	Reasonable precautions	11, 55
Denial of access	9	Rent covers	43
Departmental aspects	37	Residual value	19
Disclosure	37		
Double rent covers	43	Salvage operations	6, 7, 20
		Salvage sales	6
Electrical clause	31	Specification standard	2
Employees rights	22	Subrogation aspects	17
		Subsidiary plants	30
Finance lack of	4, 16		
Flood	31	Trend	28
Good Faith	34	Uberrimae Fides	34
		Underground workings	30
Holiday periods	4, 15	Utmost good faith	34
Hire purchase revenue	4		
		Valuation agreement	1
Interest payable	21		
		Weather effects	4, 15
Local Authorities requirements	3, 17		
Losses exclusions	9, 11		
second loss	12		
aggravated	12		